COLLEGE STUDENT HEALTH GUIDE

Managing Wellness from Freshman Year to Graduation

JULES CARSON

Copyright © 2024 by Jules Carson

All rights reserved. No part of this publication may be reproduced, distributed or transmitted in any form or by any means, including photocopying, recording, or other electronic or mechanical methods, without the prior written permission of the publisher, except in the case of brief quotations embodied in critical reviews and certain other non-commercial uses permitted by copyright law.

Trademarked names appear throughout this book. Rather than use a trademark symbol with every occurrence of a trademarked name, names are used in an editorial fashion, with no intention of infringement of the respective owner's trademark. The information in this book is distributed on an "as is" basis, without warranty. Although every precaution has been taken in the preparation of this work, neither the author nor the publisher shall have any liability to any person or entity with respect to any loss or damage caused or alleged to be caused directly or indirectly by the information contained in this book.

College is a place where you learn to take responsibility for your own life. It's a time for growing up and figuring out who you are.

— *Jeannette Walls*

Contents

Introduction: Setting the Stage for a Healthy College Life   vii

1. Building a Hygiene Routine   1
2. Eating for Energy and Wellness   15
3. Basic Medical Knowledge Every Student Should Have   26
4. Emotional Management and Mental Health   36
5. Managing College Relationships   51
6. Digital Health and Well-being   58
7. Balancing Academics and Wellness   65
8. Alcohol, Drugs, and Campus Culture   73
9. Sexual Health and Healthy Relationships   81
10. Preparing for Post-College Life   88

Conclusion: Staying Healthy for the Long Run   97

Introduction: Setting the Stage for a Healthy College Life

Welcome to college – a time of new beginnings, exciting possibilities, and endless opportunities. For many, stepping onto campus represents the first taste of independence. You're responsible for your schedule, your studies, and your social life, all while navigating a completely new environment. But amid all the excitement, one thing often gets overlooked: your health.

This guide is here to help you navigate your college years while prioritizing your well-being. The choices you make now can have a lasting impact on your physical, emotional, and mental health, not just during college but for years to come. Understanding why health matters, how to balance freedom with responsibility, and what challenges you might face is the first step to setting the stage for a successful, healthy college experience.

Why Health Matters in College

College is an incredible opportunity for personal growth, but it also comes with unique demands. With increased academic pressures, social obligations, and the need to make decisions on your own, it's easy to lose sight of the most basic aspect of self-care: your health. However, maintaining your well-being is essential for thriving in this new chapter of your life.

A healthy body supports a healthy mind. When you take care of yourself – through proper nutrition, regular physical activity, adequate sleep, and mental health practices – you're more capable of handling the academic challenges that come your way. Your concentration improves, your energy levels stay high, and your mood is more balanced. Simply put, a strong foundation of wellness helps you succeed in all areas of your life.

In college, where schedules can be unpredictable and stress is often high, the ability to care for yourself becomes even more important. The habits you develop now, from how you manage your time to how you prioritize sleep and physical activity, will shape your overall well-being for years to come. This guide is here to support you in building those habits and making your health a top priority.

Balancing Freedom with Responsibility

College also represents a major shift in personal responsibility. For the first time, you have the freedom to make your own choices about how you spend your time, what you eat, and how you manage stress. With that freedom, however, comes the responsibility to make decisions that are in your best interest, even when no one is there to remind you.

Finding balance is key. With a packed schedule of classes, extracurricular activities, and social events, it's tempting to push yourself to the limit. You might stay up late to finish assignments, skip meals to meet deadlines, or forego exercise because there just doesn't seem to be enough time. But without balance, these small sacrifices can lead to larger problems – exhaustion, burnout, or even illness.

Balancing freedom with responsibility means learning to take care of yourself while still embracing all that college has to offer. It's about making time for fun while also being mindful of your physical and mental health. This guide will walk you through how to create routines, manage stress, and set boundaries, helping you enjoy your college experience without compromising your well-being.

Common Challenges Students Face

While every student's journey is unique, there are common challenges most college students will face when it comes to health and wellness. Knowing what these challenges are can help you better prepare for them – and overcome them with confidence.

The first major challenge is time management. With a seemingly endless list of things to do, it can feel impossible to fit everything in. This guide will help you create strategies to balance academics, extracurriculars, and self-care. You'll learn how to plan your days in a way that supports your well-being, rather than drains your energy.

A second common challenge is adjusting to new eating habits. For many, college represents the first time making independent decisions about food. Whether you're navigating dining halls, cooking for yourself, or dealing with limited food budgets, figuring out how to eat well can be tricky. I'll cover tips for eating for energy and wellness, ensuring you nourish your body with what it needs to thrive.

Mental health is a third challenge faced by many college students. College brings many new pressures – social, academic, and emotional – that can take a toll on your mental well-being. It's normal to feel overwhelmed at times, but it's important to recognize when stress, anxiety, or sadness becomes more than just occasional feelings. This guide will give you tools to manage your emotional health, seek help when needed, and practice self-compassion as you navigate these challenges.

Lastly, the college environment presents unique risks when it comes to alcohol, drugs, and sexual health. Learning to navigate campus culture safely and responsibly is essential. I'll provide practical advice on how to set boundaries, make informed decisions, and ensure your safety in social situations.

Your Guide to College Wellness

This book covers everything from building a daily hygiene routine and eating for energy, to managing your mental health, navigating college relationships, and preparing for life after graduation. Each chapter is designed to give you practical advice, grounded in real-world experiences, to help you manage the specific challenges college students face.

As you read through this guide, remember that your health is not a destination – it's a lifelong journey. College is just the beginning, a time for establishing habits that will serve you well beyond graduation. By taking care of your body, mind, and relationships now, you're setting yourself up for success not only in college but in the years ahead.

Whether you're just starting your college journey or nearing the end, this guide is here to support you every step of the way. Take the time to invest in your well-being, and remember: staying healthy is the foundation for living a balanced, fulfilling, and joyful life. Welcome to the next exciting chapter of your life, and congratulations on taking the first step toward managing your wellness with confidence!

1. Building a Hygiene Routine

Your health isn't just about what you eat or how much you exercise – daily hygiene plays an equally vital role. This chapter focuses on building a solid hygiene routine that covers everything from grooming basics like hand washing, hair and skin care to the often overlooked importance of sleep and regular physical activity. You'll find practical advice on managing acne, caring for your teeth, shaving tips, and how exercise fits into maintaining your well-being. By developing these habits, you'll not only look your best but feel your best. Let's dive into how you can build a routine that supports both your health and confidence throughout college and beyond.

1. Grooming 101: From Hands to Hair and Skin Care to Acne

HAND HYGIENE

Good hand hygiene is key to staying healthy. Regular hand washing is one of the simplest and most effective ways to prevent the spread of germs and illnesses like colds, the flu, and stomach bugs.

Your hands touch many surfaces throughout the day, like door handles and phones, which can carry harmful germs. These germs can enter your body when you touch your face, especially your eyes, nose, or mouth. That's why regular handwashing is so important.

To wash your hands properly, start by wetting them with clean water and applying soap. Rub your hands together to create a lather, covering all areas: between your fingers, under your nails, around your thumbs, and even your wrists. Scrub for at least twenty seconds – singing the "ABC" song is a fun way to time it. Afterward, rinse well with water and dry your hands with a clean towel or air dry them.

If soap and water aren't available, hand sanitizer with at least 60% alcohol is a good alternative. Rub it all over your hands until they're dry, but keep in mind, sanitizers are less effective if your hands are visibly dirty or greasy.

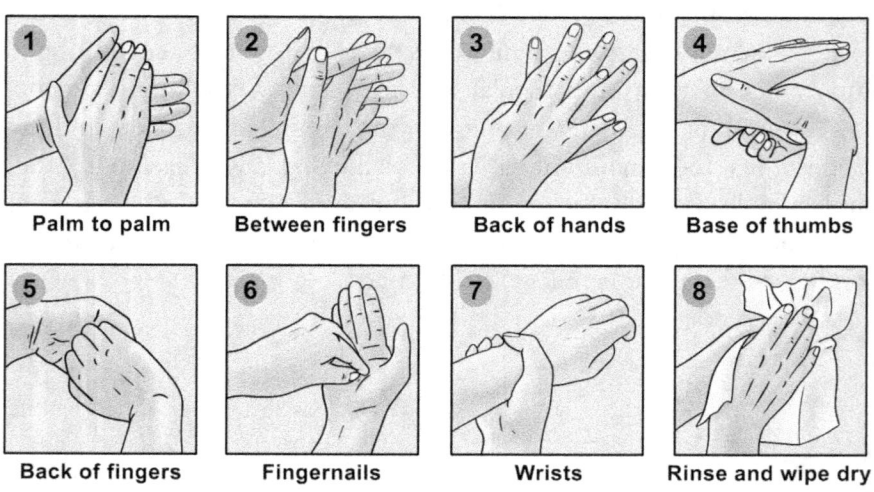

| 1. Palm to palm | 2. Between fingers | 3. Back of hands | 4. Base of thumbs |
| 5. Back of fingers | 6. Fingernails | 7. Wrists | 8. Rinse and wipe dry |

EXAMPLE SCENARIOS FOR TEENAGERS

- **Managing Breakouts Before an Exam:** You have a big exam coming up and your face breaks out. Instead of stressing over it, follow a simple skincare routine to address it. Cleanse your face with a gentle, non-comedogenic cleanser twice daily, use a topical treatment for acne, and avoid touching your face with unclean hands. Keeping a basic skincare routine can help manage and reduce breakouts, boosting your confidence during exams.
- **Handling Hair Care Between Classes:** You have a full schedule with back-to-back classes and activities. If your hair is looking greasy or flat, consider carrying a small bottle of dry shampoo or a hairbrush in your bag. A quick spray of dry shampoo can absorb excess oil and freshen up your hair, while a brush can help with any tangles. Regularly washing your hair and keeping grooming products handy will help you look and feel your best throughout the day.

HAIR CARE

Maintaining healthy hair is important for both appearance and scalp health. Whether your hair is curly, straight, thick, or thin, taking care of it can enhance its natural beauty and prevent issues like split ends, dryness, and breakage. Here are some simple tips:

1. Choose the Right Products: Use shampoos and conditioners suited to your hair type. Moisturizing products are great for dry hair, while those with oily hair should opt for balancing or volumizing options.

2. Washing Routine: Avoid daily washing, as it strips natural oils. Wash your hair every two to three days, and use lukewarm water to prevent dryness.

3. Proper Conditioning: Always condition the ends of your hair after washing, letting it sit for a few minutes before rinsing.

4. Drying Techniques: Minimize the use of heat styling tools. If you must use a dryer, keep it on a low setting and hold it away from your hair. Air drying is a healthier option when possible.

5. Regular Trimming: Trim your hair every six to eight weeks to prevent split ends and encourage healthy growth.

6. Diet and Hydration: A balanced diet rich in vitamins, minerals, and omega-3 fatty acids supports strong, shiny hair. Staying hydrated is essential for overall hair health.

7. Protective Hairstyles: Loose buns or braids can protect long hair from breakage and tangles.

Skin Care

Proper skin care is key to keeping your skin healthy and looking its best. Whether you have oily, dry, or combination skin, using the right products consistently can help you achieve a clear and glowing complexion. The three most important steps in any routine are cleansing, moisturizing, and protecting your skin from the sun. This guide will help you incorporate these essential practices into your daily routine and understand how they benefit your skin.

Before starting a skincare routine, it's important to know your skin type. This will help you choose the right products and approach to maintaining balanced skin. There are five main skin types: normal, oily, dry, combination, and sensitive. Each type has its own characteristics and requires specific care.

1. Normal Skin: This skin type is balanced, neither too oily nor too dry. It typically has few imperfections and a smooth texture. A simple skincare routine focused on maintaining its natural balance works best for normal skin.

2. Oily Skin: Oily skin often appears shiny, has large pores, and is prone to acne and blackheads. This type benefits from products that regulate oil without stripping the skin, such as gel-based cleansers and lightweight moisturizers.

3. Dry Skin: Dry skin feels tight and may flake or itch. It often shows more visible lines and has less elasticity. Rich, emollient products that deeply hydrate and lock in moisture are essential for dry skin.

4. Combination Skin: This type features both oily and dry areas, typically with oiliness in the T-zone (forehead, nose, and chin) and dryness on the cheeks. A balanced routine that addresses both needs is key, sometimes requiring different products for different areas of the face.

5. Sensitive Skin: Sensitive skin is easily irritated by products or environmental factors and may show redness, itching, or dryness. It needs gentle, fragrance-free products designed for sensitive skin to prevent reactions.

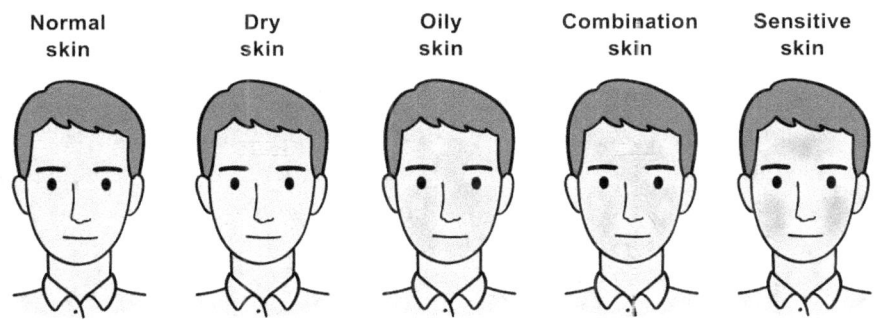

To determine your skin type, start with a clean face and observe how your skin behaves after a few hours without any products. Focus on how it feels, especially in different areas like the forehead and cheeks. This simple test will help guide your product choices.

An effective skincare routine includes the following steps:

1. Cleansing: Cleansing is the first and most important step, as it removes dirt, oil, and impurities from the skin. Choose a cleanser that suits your skin type. Oily skin benefits from foaming or gel-based cleansers, while dry skin needs creamier, hydrating options. Cleanse your face twice daily, once in the morning and again at night, to keep pores clear and your skin refreshed.

2. Moisturizing: After cleansing, always apply a moisturizer. This helps lock in moisture and keep the skin soft, preventing dryness. Select a moisturizer based on your skin type. Oily skin benefits from lightweight, oil-free products, while dry skin may need a richer, cream-based moisturizer. Even if your skin is oily, don't skip this step – hydration is crucial for all skin types.

3. Sun Protection: Protecting your skin from the sun is one of the most important things you can do. Harmful UV (ultraviolet) rays can cause premature aging and increase the risk of skin cancer. Use a broad-spectrum sunscreen with an SPF (Sun Protection Factor) of at least thirty every day, even when it's cloudy. Apply generously to all exposed skin, and reapply every two hours, especially if you're swimming or sweating.

Acne

Acne is a common skin condition that affects people of all ages, particularly teenagers and young adults. It happens when hair follicles get clogged with oil and dead skin cells, leading to whiteheads, blackheads, or pimples. Factors like hormonal changes, diet, stress, and improper skincare can make acne worse. Here are some effective ways to manage it:

1. Gentle Cleansing: Wash your face gently twice a day with a mild, non-comedogenic cleanser to avoid clogging pores. Avoid harsh scrubbing, as it can irritate your skin and worsen acne. Use your fingers to apply the cleanser in circular motions, and rinse with lukewarm water.

2. Topical Treatments: Over-the-counter treatments with ingredients like benzoyl peroxide, salicylic acid, or retinoids can help reduce acne by controlling oil production and fighting bacteria.

3. Moisturize: Many acne treatments dry out the skin, so it's essential to use a non-comedogenic moisturizer to keep your skin hydrated and prevent irritation.

4. Avoid Touching and Picking: Try not to touch or pick at your acne, as this can lead to more inflammation and potential scarring. Keeping your hands off your face also reduces the spread of bacteria.

5. Consider Your Diet: Some studies suggest that foods like sugar and dairy may trigger acne. Dairy, in particular, contains hormones that could increase oil production. Try eliminating dairy for a week to see if your skin improves.

6. Manage Stress: High stress levels can worsen acne by increasing cortisol, a hormone linked to breakouts. Engage in stress-relieving activities like meditation or exercise to help control stress.

7. Clean Bedding: Change your pillowcases regularly, at least every four days, to avoid the buildup of oils and dirt that can contribute to acne. You can also cover your pillow with a clean cotton t-shirt and flip it daily for a fresh surface.

8. See a Dermatologist: If acne persists or becomes severe, consult a dermatologist. Prescription treatments may be needed to manage tougher cases.

Shaving

Shaving is a common practice for both men and women, typically involving the face, legs, and underarms. Using proper techniques can help prevent skin irritation, razor burn, and ingrown hairs. Here are some key tips for effective shaving:

1. Preparation: Before shaving, soften the hair and prepare the skin. A warm shower or bath helps open pores, making the hair easier to remove. Alternatively, use a warm, damp towel on the area for a few minutes before shaving.

2. Use a Clean, Sharp Razor: A sharp blade ensures a smoother shave and lowers the risk of nicks and cuts. Dull razors can pull at hair, causing irritation. Replace blades regularly, about every five to ten shaves, to maintain sharpness.

3. Shaving Cream or Gel: Apply a generous amount of shaving cream or gel. These products hydrate the hair, making it easier to cut, and provide a barrier that allows the razor to glide smoothly over the skin, reducing irritation.

4. Proper Technique: Shave in the direction of hair growth to avoid irritation and ingrown hairs. For a closer shave, carefully shave against the grain on a second pass. Use gentle strokes and let the razor do the work.

5. Aftercare: Rinse with cool water after shaving to close pores, and apply a hydrating aftershave lotion or balm. Avoid alcohol-based aftershaves as they can dry out the skin. Products with aloe are great for soothing sensitive areas.

6. Skin Care: For sensitive skin, use hypoallergenic products. Regular exfoliation (but not right before shaving) can help prevent ingrown hairs by removing dead skin cells.

Here is an image illustrating the optimal directions for shaving your face. Following these directions helps achieve a closer shave while minimizing irritation and the risk of ingrown hairs.

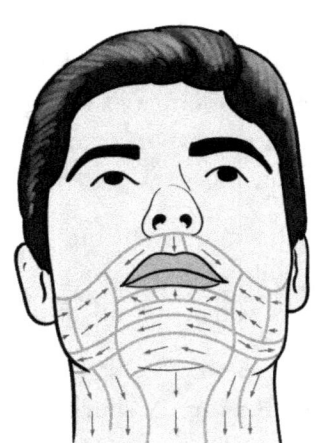

2. Oral Hygiene: More Than Just Brushing

Good oral hygiene is essential for overall health and confidence. This section offers tips on maintaining a healthy mouth, fresh breath, and a bright smile.

1. Brushing Techniques: Effective brushing techniques are the cornerstone of good oral hygiene. Brush your teeth at least twice a day, preferably after meals. Use a soft-bristled toothbrush and replace it every three months or when the bristles fray. Hold the brush at a forty-five degree angle to your gums, using gentle, circular motions. Brush all surfaces of your teeth, including the fronts, backs, and chewing surfaces, for at least two minutes. It's best to brush after breakfast and dinner to remove food particles and plaque.

2. Flossing: Floss daily to clean between your teeth where a brush can't reach. Use about eighteen inches (forty-five centimeters) of floss, wrap it around your middle fingers, and gently slide it between each tooth. Curve the floss into a C shape against each tooth and use a clean section for each one.

3. Choosing Toothpaste: Select a fluoride toothpaste to strengthen enamel and prevent cavities. If you have concerns like sensitivity or tartar buildup, choose a specialized toothpaste. Avoid abrasive toothpaste, as it can wear down enamel.

4. Mouthwash: Mouthwash can reduce plaque, fight bacteria, and freshen breath. Use a fluoride mouthwash for extra cavity protection, swishing for about thirty seconds before spitting it out.

5. Regular Dental Check-ups: Visit your dentist every six months for cleanings and check-ups. Regular visits catch problems like cavities and gum disease early. Professional cleanings remove plaque and tartar that brushing and flossing can't eliminate.

6. Diet: Limit sugary and acidic foods and drinks to prevent tooth decay. A balanced diet rich in fruits, vegetables, proteins, and dairy supports oral health.

7. Tobacco: Avoid tobacco, as it can cause gum disease, tooth decay, and oral cancer, and lead to bad breath and stained teeth.

8. Special Considerations: For braces, use an orthodontic toothbrush and floss threaders. Clean removable appliances like retainers regularly to prevent bacteria buildup.

Managing common issues like tooth sensitivity, dry mouth, and bad breath can also help maintain a healthy smile. Use specialized toothpaste, stay hydrated, and maintain good hygiene habits.

Example Scenarios for Teenagers

- **Snacking During Study Sessions:** If you snack on sugary treats during long study sessions, and you don't clean your teeth afterward, the sugar can stick to your teeth and result in cavities. Make it a habit to rinse your mouth with water after eating, especially if you can't brush right away. Try to floss daily too, especially after meals, to remove food particles that brushing might miss. Small actions like these can go a long way in keeping your teeth and gums in good shape throughout college.
- **Prepping for a Big Presentation:** Let's say you have an important presentation in class. You want to make a good impression, so you ensure your appearance is sharp, but bad breath could throw you off your game. The night before, brush your teeth, floss, and rinse with mouthwash to eliminate any food particles and bacteria that cause odor. In the morning, brush your tongue along with your teeth, and carry a small travel-sized mouthwash or pack of mints to freshen up before your presentation. A healthy oral care routine will help you feel more confident.

3. The Power of Sleep: How Rest Impacts Your Health

Sleep is essential for your health and well-being, yet it's often neglected. Did you know that sleep impacts nearly every system in the body, from your brain and heart to your mood and immune function? As such, getting adequate sleep helps with heart and blood vessel repair, hormone balance, growth, and stress response. It also boosts concentration, productivity, and performance.

Teens need around eight to nine hours of sleep per night, but only 3% get enough. Lack of sleep can harm school performance, mood, and increase the risk of accidents and health problems like obesity and diabetes.

Improving sleep quality may seem overwhelming, but small changes can make a big difference. Start with your sleep environment. A cool, dark, and quiet room can significantly improve your sleep. Lower your bedroom temperature, minimize noise, and make your room as dark as possible by closing blinds and removing light-emitting electronics.

Here are some other effective strategies you can implement to improve your sleep quality:

1. Optimize Your Bedroom Setup: Move phone and laptop chargers across the room to keep lights and screens out of reach. This not only eliminates distractions but also forces you to get up to turn off your alarm, reducing the temptation to hit snooze.

2. Establish a Sleep Routine: Consistency is key. Go to bed and wake up at the same time each day to train your body's internal clock. Instead of using screens before bed, try relaxing activities like reading or listening to calming music.

3. Adjust Lighting and Electronics: Dim lights and warmer hues signal your body to produce melatonin, which helps you sleep. Switch to softer lighting in the evening, and use your phone's 'night shift' feature to reduce blue light exposure.

4. Dietary Adjustments: Also, avoid large meals before bedtime so your body can focus on resting rather than digestion.

5. Sleep Aids: Weighted blankets can help by applying gentle pressure that relaxes the body. Sleep tracking devices like Fitbit or Oura Ring can also offer insights into your sleep patterns, helping you make informed adjustments.

Prioritizing sleep can improve your memory, mood, grades, athletic performance, and immune system. It's one of the simplest ways to enhance your overall well-being, leading to noticeable improvements in many areas of your life. Make sleep a priority, and you'll quickly see the positive effects on both your physical and mental health.

Example Scenarios for Teenagers

- **Balancing Late-Night Study Sessions:** Imagine you have a big exam coming up and find yourself studying late into the night. To manage this, set a specific end time for your study session, ideally two hours before you plan to sleep. This helps your brain unwind and prepares your body for rest. Try to create a bedtime routine that includes winding down with a book or some calming music instead of screen time to enhance your sleep quality and help you feel more refreshed.
- **Recovering from a Busy Week:** If you are exhausted after a week full of late nights and early mornings, plan a weekend where you prioritize getting extra sleep. Use this time to catch up on rest and establish a regular sleep schedule, aiming for seven to nine hours of quality sleep each night. This can help restore your energy levels and improve your focus and mood, setting you up for a more balanced and productive week ahead.

4. Physical Activity: Finding Time to Exercise

Exercise is a vital part of a healthy lifestyle, benefiting both physical and mental health. Regular activity helps maintain a healthy weight, reduces the risk of chronic diseases like heart disease and diabetes, and strengthens bones and muscles. Beyond the physical benefits, exercise improves mental well-being by reducing symptoms of depression and anxiety, lifting mood, and boosting cognitive function. For teenagers, exercise supports growth and development while encouraging lifelong wellness habits.

Exercise can be broken down into several types, each contributing to overall fitness. Aerobic exercises like jogging, swimming, cycling, and walking improve cardiovascular health and stamina by increasing heart rate and circulation. Strength training, using weights or body-weight exercises like push-ups and squats, builds muscle and strengthens bones. Flexibility exercises such as yoga or stretching improve joint mobility and muscle elasticity. Combining these types of exercises leads to optimal fitness.

Here are some tips to get started:

1. Set Realistic Goals: Begin with manageable targets and increase intensity as you progress.

2. Find Activities You Enjoy: Discovering enjoyable exercises makes it easier to stick to a routine.

3. Create a Routine: Schedule exercise sessions as important appointments.

4. Mix It Up: Vary activities to keep things interesting and engage different muscle groups.

5. Exercise with Friends or Family: Working out with others adds fun and motivation.

6. Track Your Progress: Keeping a record of your achievements helps maintain motivation and a sense of accomplishment.

EXAMPLE SCENARIOS FOR TEENAGERS

- **Finding Time Between Classes:** If there's a weekday where you have a long break between your morning and afternoon classes, use this time for a quick workout – whether it's a brisk walk around campus, a short jog, or a twenty-minute bodyweight exercise routine. You can even find a spot to do some stretching or yoga. Integrating these short bursts of activity into your schedule helps you stay active without needing to carve out extra time.

- **Making Exercise a Social Activity:** Imagine you're trying to stay active but struggle to fit it into your busy schedule. Join a campus fitness club or group exercise class that meets regularly. This way, you can combine socializing with staying fit. Whether it's a dance class, a sports team, or a fitness group, having a scheduled activity with friends can make exercising fun and easier to stick with, turning it into a positive part of your routine.

2. Eating for Energy and Wellness

Nourishing your body with the right foods is essential for maintaining energy, focus, and overall well-being, especially during the busy college years. In this chapter, you'll discover practical strategies for eating healthy, even on a tight budget. From smart grocery shopping tips to meal planning ideas tailored for busy students, you'll learn how to make nutritious choices that fit your lifestyle. Staying hydrated is equally important, and I'll explain why water is your best ally in maintaining peak performance. Whether you're cooking for the first time or refining your eating habits, this chapter provides the tools you need to create meals that support both your health and your academic success.

1. Healthy Eating on a Budget

Starting college often means learning to balance many new responsibilities, including managing your meals. Eating well is crucial for maintaining energy, focus, and overall well-being, but with a limited budget, it can sometimes feel challenging. The good news is that you can maintain a nutritious diet without breaking the bank by being mindful of your choices and focusing on affordable, healthy options.

Here are some tips to help you eat well on a budget:

1. **Choose Whole Foods Over Processed Foods:** While pre-packaged and processed foods may seem convenient, they often cost more in the long run and lack essential nutrients. Whole foods like fruits, vegetables, grains, and legumes are not only healthier but also more affordable. Opt for items like brown rice, oats, beans, and seasonal produce to get more nutrients for your dollar.

2. **Buy in Bulk:** Purchasing items like grains, lentils, nuts, and seeds in bulk can significantly reduce costs. These foods are not only inexpensive but also have a long shelf life, making them perfect for stocking up without worrying about them spoiling. Bulk purchases are often much cheaper per serving compared to smaller packages.

3. **Incorporate Plant-Based Proteins:** Meat can be expensive, especially on a student budget. Consider incorporating plant-based protein sources like beans, lentils, tofu, and chickpeas into your meals. These foods are nutrient-dense, cost-effective, and versatile, allowing you to create a variety of satisfying dishes.

4. **Avoid Eating Out Regularly:** While grabbing takeout or eating at a restaurant is tempting, it can quickly add up. Eating out regularly can strain your budget and often leads to less healthy choices. Save dining out for special occasions and focus on preparing meals at home whenever possible.

5. **Stay Hydrated with Water:** Soft drinks, juices, and specialty coffees are not only expensive but often packed with sugar and empty calories. Instead, make water your go-to drink. It's free (if you're using

tap water) and essential for your health. If you want a bit of flavor, try adding slices of lemon, cucumber, or mint to your water.

By following these tips, you can nourish your body, stay within your budget, and still enjoy a variety of delicious and healthy meals.

It's recommended to eat three balanced meals and one or two healthy snacks (in between meals) every day to keep your energy up and your body feeling its best. Try not to skip meals, especially not breakfast, as it can lead to overeating later. Additionally, sticking to regular meal times can support your digestion and help you feel more balanced and focused throughout the day.

Eating well in college doesn't have to be complicated or expensive – it just requires a bit of discipline, creativity and smart choices.

EXAMPLE SCENARIOS FOR TEENAGERS

- **Making Smart Choices at the Grocery Store:** Let's say you have $30 for the week's groceries. Instead of buying expensive pre-packaged meals, focus on basics like rice, pasta, beans, and frozen vegetables. These ingredients are affordable, last longer, and can be used to make multiple meals. Look for store brands or items on sale, and try to plan meals that stretch your budget, like a big batch of chili or pasta that can last several days.
- **Eating Well with Limited Time and Money:** If you're pressed for time between classes, instead of grabbing fast food, prepare simple meals like a sandwich with whole-grain bread, a boiled egg, and some fruit. It's cheaper and healthier than eating out, and preparing meals at home helps you stay on budget while nourishing your body with the right nutrients.

2. Smart Grocery Shopping: Tips for Beginners

Grocery shopping requires a bit of planning and knowledge to choose the best products for both health and value. Here's a guide to help you make smart choices when buying fruits, vegetables, proteins, cheese, and bread.

FRUITS AND VEGETABLES

Fruits and vegetables are essential for a nutritious diet, providing vitamins, minerals, and fiber. Prioritize seasonal produce for freshness and better prices, and choose local and organic when possible. However, non-organic is still better than not consuming any fruits and vegetables at all.

Aim for a variety of colors in your selection, as different colors offer diverse nutrients and antioxidants. Ripe fruits are ideal – they have better flavor, peak nutrient levels, and are easier to juice. By focusing on seasonal, colorful, and ripe produce, you can improve the nutritional value of your diet.

Apple — Skin is firm to the touch with little to no bruises

Cherry — Firm flesh, Attached stem

Strawberry — No white or green near leaves, Dark green leaves not dried out

Tomato — 90% red surface

Avocados — Brown-green skin

Mango — Smells sweet at stem, Slight indent when pressed

Orange — Firm skin that doesn't feel leathery

Pineapple — 100% yellow skin

Grape — Firm and plump on all sides

Kiwi — Slight give when gently pressed

Pear — Slight give when gently pressed near the stem

Watermelon — Dark and dull rind, Tan field spot, firm skin

Fish and Meats

Proteins like fish and meats are crucial for building tissues, making enzymes, and maintaining bone health. When buying fish, choose wild-caught over farmed to reduce exposure to contaminants. For chicken and beef, opt for organic, free-range, or grass-fed varieties, which typically indicate higher quality and better animal welfare.

Freshness is key – look for firm texture and consistent color, and always check sell-by dates. Proper storage is essential too – keep proteins refrigerated or frozen and plan meals to use them soon after purchase to maintain freshness.

Cheese and Bread

Cheese, rich in calcium, protein, and fat, is a versatile addition to any diet. Experiment with different types for new flavors. For bread, whole-grain varieties are best, offering more nutrients and fiber than white or refined types, supporting digestion and stable blood sugar levels.

When buying cheese and bread, read labels carefully to avoid additives like high fructose corn syrup or growth hormones, ensuring you make healthier choices.

Example Scenarios for Teenagers

- **Starting with a List:** Imagine it's your first time grocery shopping for yourself. Before heading to the store, make a list of the essentials – things like milk, eggs, whole grains, and fresh or frozen vegetables. This will keep you focused and help you avoid impulse buys. Stick to the perimeter of the store where most fresh foods are found, and try to skip the snack aisle unless it's on your list. A well-planned list can save you money and prevent waste.
- **Comparing Prices and Choosing Wisely:** While shopping, you notice two different brands of pasta – one is a well-known name, and the other is a store brand that costs a

dollar less. Choosing the store brand can help you stick to your budget while still getting a quality product. Small choices like this add up, helping you stay financially savvy without compromising on what you need.

3. Reading Food Labels: Decoding Food Packaging Information

Nutritional labels provide detailed information about the nutritional content of foods, helping you to evaluate their health benefits and risks.

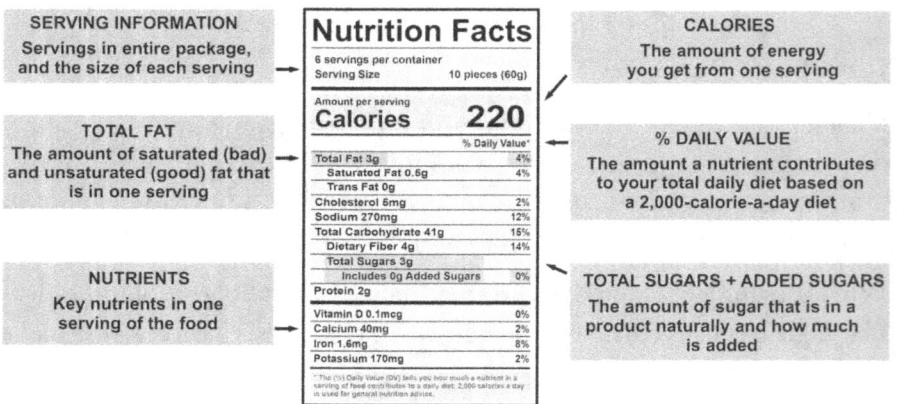

1. Serving Size: This is listed at the top and is important because all the other information is based on this amount. Be sure to check how much you actually eat. If you consume more than the listed serving, you're also taking in more calories, fat, sugar, etc.

2. Calories: This shows the total calories per serving. Keeping track of calorie intake is essential for managing a healthy weight.

3. Macronutrients:

- **Total Fat**: Includes saturated, unsaturated, and trans fats. Choose foods low in saturated and trans fats for better heart health.

- **Cholesterol and Sodium**: High levels can contribute to heart issues and high blood pressure, so it's important to limit these.
- **Carbohydrates**: This includes fiber and sugar. Look for foods with high fiber and low sugar for a healthier diet.

4. Vitamins and Minerals: Nutrients like vitamin A, calcium, and iron are listed as a percentage of daily needs. Aim to meet these daily values.

5. Percent Daily Values (%DV): This indicates how much of a nutrient one serving contributes to a 2,000-calorie diet. A %DV of 5% or less is low, while 20% or more is high.

Example Scenarios for Teenagers

- **Understanding Sugar Content:** You're craving a quick snack between classes and decide to grab a granola bar at the campus convenience store. Before buying it, check the nutritional label for added sugars. If the label shows twelve grams of sugar in a single serving and you aim to reduce sugar, you might choose a healthier option with lower sugar content.

- **Choosing Low Sodium Meals:** While shopping for dinner ingredients, you pick up a can of soup. The label shows 900 mg of sodium per serving, which is almost 40% of your daily recommended intake. If you're trying to reduce sodium, you might opt for a low-sodium version or make homemade soup instead.

4. Meal Planning for Busy Students

Meal planning is a helpful strategy for organizing your meals for the week, day, or month. It involves selecting recipes, shopping for ingredients, and sometimes prepping meals ahead of time. This approach simplifies your routine and ensures a balanced, nutritious diet.

The benefits of meal planning are numerous. First, it helps save money by reducing impulse purchases and making better use of what's already in your pantry. Planning ahead also saves time, as you spend less energy deciding what to eat each day or making last-minute trips to the store. Additionally, it promotes healthier eating by allowing you to thoughtfully plan a well-rounded menu that incorporates a variety of food groups. By buying only what you need, meal planning reduces food waste, and it also reduces the stress of figuring out meals on the fly, helping to alleviate decision fatigue. Together, these advantages make meal planning a smart way to manage both your budget and your health.

To start meal planning, begin by reviewing your schedule for the week. On busy days, choose quick and easy meals, while saving more complex recipes for when you have more time. Try adding variety by incorporating themed nights like "Meatless Monday" or "Taco Tuesday." Once you've selected your recipes, make a shopping list to keep your grocery trip efficient. Prepping ingredients in advance, such as chopping vegetables or marinating proteins, can also help cut down daily prep time. Store your meals or components in clear, labeled containers with cooking instructions or 'use-by' dates to stay organized.

To make meal planning easier and more fun, consider using apps that store recipes, generate shopping lists, and suggest meals based on what you have at home like Mealime or Yummly. Batch cooking is another time-saving strategy – by preparing large quantities of ingredients like grilled chicken or roasted vegetables, you can mix and match them in different meals throughout the week. Lastly, stay flexible with a few backup meals, such as frozen veggie burgers or easy pantry recipes like canned soup with a grilled cheese, to handle unexpected changes in your schedule.

By following these steps, meal planning can save you time, reduce stress, and improve your eating habits, making your life easier and healthier.

EXAMPLE SCENARIOS FOR TEENAGERS

- **Weekly Meal Prep:** Imagine you have a busy week ahead with classes and study sessions. To make mealtime easier, dedicate a few hours on the weekend to meal prep. Cook a batch of brown rice, roast some chicken, and prepare a big salad. Portion these into containers so you have ready-to-go meals throughout the week. This way, you'll save time and avoid the temptation of unhealthy fast food.
- **Quick and Easy Dinners:** Suppose you have a hectic day with back-to-back classes. For a quick dinner, keep ingredients like canned beans, frozen vegetables, and whole-grain tortillas on hand. You can quickly make a nutritious wrap or stir-fry. Having these versatile staples means you can whip up a healthy meal in minutes, even when your schedule is packed.

5. Water and Hydration: Staying Fueled All Day

Hydration is essential for good health, as a significant part of our bodies – 55-60% in adults and around 75% in infants – is made up of water. Water plays a key role in many bodily functions: it cushions joints, regulates body temperature, and supports brain and spinal cord health. Staying hydrated is crucial for these processes and for overall well-being.

Water is found throughout the body, including vital organs like the brain and heart (which are about 75% water) and even bones, which are around 30% water. We lose between half a gallon (1.9 liters) to nearly a gallon (3.8 liters) of water each day through sweat, urine, and bowel movements. Replenishing this lost fluid is necessary to prevent dehydration.

Dehydration can affect energy, mood, skin, blood pressure, and cognitive function. The brain, in particular, works harder when dehydrated and can even shrink temporarily due to water loss.

Daily water needs vary by age, sex, and activity level. On average, men need about 125 ounces (3.7 liters) of fluids per day, while women require about ninety-one ounces (2.7 liters). About 20% of our daily fluid intake comes from food, and drinks like coffee and tea also contribute to hydration.

To stay hydrated, carry a water bottle with you throughout the day, making it easier to drink regularly. Include water-rich foods like fruits and vegetables in your diet to boost hydration. If plain water feels boring, add slices of fruit or a splash of juice for flavor. Set reminders or mark your water bottle with time intervals to track your progress and ensure you're drinking enough water consistently. These simple strategies can help you stay properly hydrated.

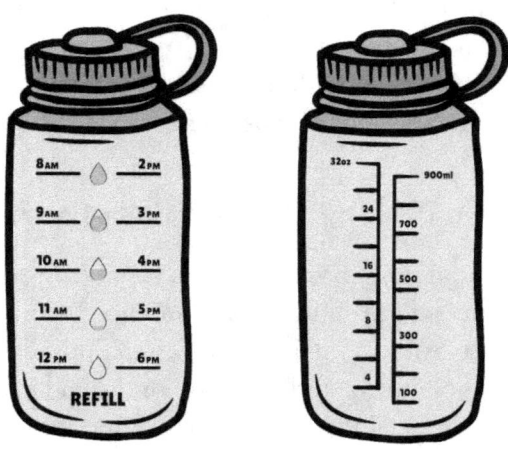

Example Scenarios for Teenagers

- **Busy Class Schedule:** If your day is packed with back-to-back classes, it's easy to forget to drink water. Carry a refillable water bottle with you and make it a habit to take sips between classes or during breaks. Staying hydrated will help you stay focused and energized throughout the day.
- **Caffeine vs. Water:** If you're relying on coffee or energy drinks to stay awake during long study sessions, remember that these can dehydrate you. For every cup of coffee, drink a glass of water to maintain your hydration levels. This balance helps you stay alert without the crash that can come from too much caffeine.

3. Basic Medical Knowledge Every Student Should Have

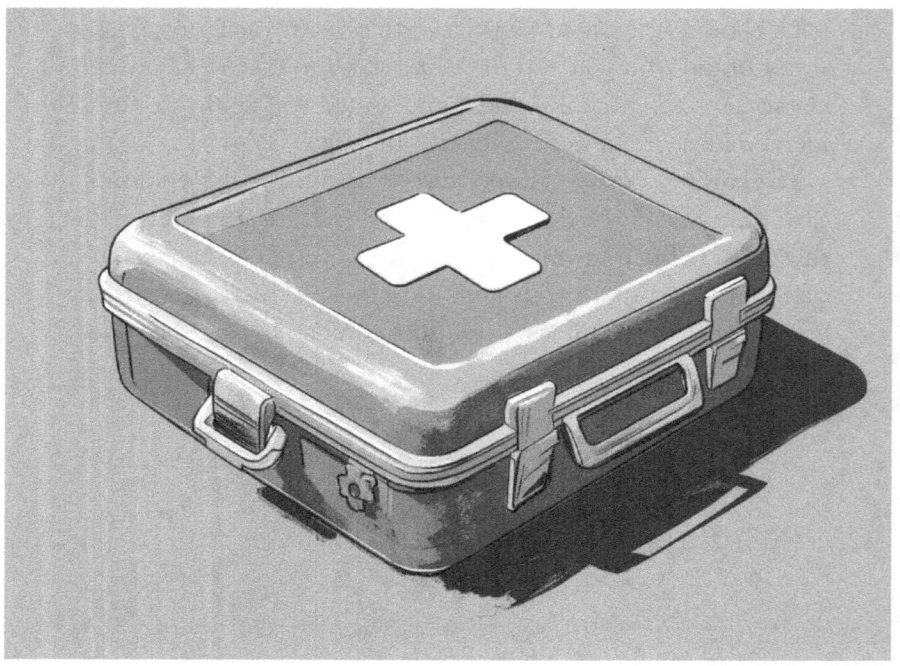

Understanding basic medical knowledge is a vital part of staying healthy, especially when living away from home for the first time. This chapter provides you with essential information to handle common health concerns that may arise during college life. From managing minor injuries with first aid to knowing how to care for yourself during a cold or flu, you'll learn practical tips for staying well. Recognizing serious symptoms and knowing when to seek professional help is just as important, and I'll also cover life-saving skills like Cardiopulmonary Resuscitation (CPR) and stroke awareness. With this knowledge, you'll feel more confident in taking charge of your health and knowing how to respond in any situation.

1. First Aid 101: Handling Minor Injuries

First aid skills are essential for everyone, not just those pursuing medical careers. As a teenager, learning these skills prepares you to handle minor injuries and emergencies, whether at home, school, or during activities.

Cuts and Scrapes

Cuts and scrapes are common and require prompt attention to prevent infection. Begin by gently rinsing the wound with lukewarm water to remove dirt. Use mild soap around the wound but avoid applying it directly to avoid irritation. After cleaning, apply a thin layer of antibiotic ointment, such as Neosporin, to prevent infection. Then, cover the wound with a sterile bandage or gauze. Change the bandage daily or sooner if it becomes wet or dirty. This helps create an optimal environment for healing.

Minor Burns

Minor burns from heat, steam, or chemicals need immediate care. First, cool the burn under cool, running water or apply a cool, wet cloth for ten to fifteen minutes to reduce pain and inflammation. After cooling, cover the burn with a sterile, non-adhesive bandage. Ensure it's wrapped loosely to avoid pressure on the sensitive area. Avoid using ice, creams, or butter, as they can restrict blood flow or cause infection.

Sprained Ankles

Sprained ankles are common among active teenagers. To treat a sprain, start with rest and avoid putting weight on the ankle. Apply ice wrapped in a towel for twenty minutes every two hours to reduce swelling. Use an elastic bandage for gentle compression, but ensure it's not too tight. Elevating the ankle above heart level can also help reduce swelling.

Nosebleeds

Nosebleeds, while usually not serious, can be distressing. Sit upright to lower blood pressure in the nasal veins and lean forward slightly to avoid swallowing blood. Pinch the soft part of your nose for at least ten minutes to help clot the blood. Breathe through your mouth to stay calm. Avoid lying down or tilting your head back, as this can cause blood to flow down your throat, which can lead to coughing or choking.

Bee Stings

Bee stings are painful and can trigger allergic reactions in some people. First, remove the stinger by scraping it out with a rigid object, like a credit card, to minimize venom entering the body. Apply ice to reduce swelling and pain, using brief intervals of fifteen minutes on and off. If there's significant swelling or itching, an over-the-counter antihistamine may help alleviate symptoms.

Learning these simple first aid techniques can make a big difference in managing common injuries and preventing further complications.

Example Scenarios for Teenagers

- **Treating a Cut During Group Study:** You're in a group study session, and someone accidentally cuts their finger while using scissors. Instead of panicking, calmly clean the wound with water, apply an antiseptic, and cover it with a bandage. Keeping a small first aid kit in your backpack can help you handle minor injuries like this.
- **Managing a Sprain on Campus:** You twist your ankle while running on a treadmill in the campus gym. First, find a place to sit and elevate your foot. Ask your friend, gym buddy or someone to get you a cold pack or some ice wrapped in a towel and apply it to your ankle to reduce swelling. Remember to keep weight off the injury. Knowing basic first aid for sprains can prevent further injury and help you recover faster.

2. Cold, Flu, and Fever: How to Manage at Home

Colds and flu are common respiratory illnesses that most people will experience several times in their lives. While both can often be managed at home, knowing how to care for yourself properly can shorten your illness and prevent spreading it to others.

Both the cold and flu are caused by different viruses but share similar symptoms, such as coughing, sneezing, sore throat, and sometimes fever. The flu is typically more severe, often including body aches and significant fatigue. Recognizing these differences can help guide your self-care and determine when to seek medical advice.

1. Rest: Resting is crucial, as your body needs energy to fight off the virus. Aim for plenty of sleep and avoid unnecessary physical activity.

2. Hydration: Drink plenty of fluids like water, herbal teas, and broths to stay hydrated and thin mucus. Avoid alcohol and caffeine, as they can dehydrate you.

3. Nutrition: Eating nutritious, light meals can help you recover faster. Focus on fruits, vegetables, and proteins, and opt for warm meals, which are easier to digest. Chicken soup can be especially soothing.

4. Soothing Symptoms: Over-the-counter medications like acetaminophen or ibuprofen can help reduce fever and ease body aches. Throat lozenges and saline nasal sprays can relieve a sore throat and congestion. Always follow dosage instructions or consult a healthcare professional.

5. Humidity: Dry air can worsen respiratory symptoms, so using a humidifier in your room can help ease congestion and coughing.

6. Isolation: To avoid spreading the virus, try to stay away from others, especially during the first few days when you're most contagious.

7. When to Seek Medical Attention: See a doctor if symptoms last more than a week, if you have severe symptoms like difficulty breathing, chest pain, or if your fever returns after breaking.

Having a well-stocked medical kit at home is also essential for managing colds, flu, and minor illnesses. Your kit should include basic first aid supplies like bandages, antiseptic wipes, and adhesive tape for small injuries. A thermometer is useful for monitoring fevers, which are common with colds and flu. Keep pain relievers like ibuprofen or acetaminophen to manage fever and aches, and stock up on cold and flu medications, including decongestants, cough suppressants, and throat lozenges.

Antihistamines (a medicine that reduces allergy symptoms like sneezing and itching by blocking a chemical called histamine) can help with allergies, while hydration salts can prevent dehydration during fever or gastrointestinal upset. Anti-diarrheal medications are useful for managing diarrhea that can accompany other illnesses, and antacids can soothe upset stomachs.

For hygiene, have hand sanitizer and disposable gloves to reduce the spread of germs, particularly when caring for someone sick. Also, keep a list of emergency contacts, including your doctor, local emergency services, and nearby hospitals. Ensure your medical kit is accessible and check it regularly to replace expired or used-up items. Taking these steps can help you manage health issues at home effectively.

Example Scenarios for Teenagers

- **Dealing with a Cold Before Exams:** If you catch a cold during exam week, prioritize rest to allow your body to heal. Drink plenty of fluids, like water or herbal tea, and use over-the-counter medicine to relieve symptoms. Create a study schedule that includes breaks for rest, and avoid pushing yourself too hard. Taking care of your health will help you recover faster and be more prepared for your exams.
- **Coping with Cold Symptoms in Class:** You wake up with a stuffy nose and sore throat but still need to attend class. Carry tissues, drink warm fluids, and use cough drops to soothe your throat. Keeping yourself hydrated and prepared can help you

manage symptoms and get through the day without feeling too uncomfortable.

3. Recognizing Serious Symptoms: When to Seek Medical Help

As a college student, it's important to know when to seek medical help. While many minor illnesses can be managed with rest, hydration, and over-the-counter medications, some symptoms shouldn't be ignored. Recognizing when you need to see a healthcare professional can make a big difference in your recovery and overall health.

Here are some signs and symptoms that may require prompt medical attention:

1. High Fever: If your temperature rises above 103°F (39.4°C) or if a lower fever lasts for more than a few days, it's important to see a doctor. A persistent fever could be a sign of an infection that requires medical treatment.

2. Difficulty Breathing: Shortness of breath, wheezing, or chest tightness are symptoms that need immediate medical attention. These could indicate asthma, a respiratory infection, or something more serious, like pneumonia.

3. Severe or Persistent Pain: Whether it's in your abdomen, chest, or head, sharp or ongoing pain is a red flag. Sudden chest pain, especially if accompanied by nausea, sweating, or dizziness, could signal a heart issue and requires urgent care.

4. Unexplained Weight Loss: Losing a significant amount of weight without trying can be a symptom of an underlying health problem. If you're noticing drastic weight changes, it's a good idea to check in with a healthcare provider.

5. Prolonged Fatigue: If you're constantly feeling tired despite getting enough sleep, this could be a sign of something more serious, like anemia, depression, or a thyroid problem. Fatigue that persists for weeks should be discussed with a doctor.

6. Changes in Mental Health: Feeling anxious, hopeless, or experiencing extreme mood swings can sometimes signal a mental health issue that requires professional support. If you're feeling overwhelmed, it's important to reach out to a counselor or health provider.

7. Persistent Vomiting or Diarrhea: If you can't keep food or fluids down, or if vomiting or diarrhea lasts more than a day or two, you risk dehydration. Seek help if this happens, especially if you also feel weak or dizzy.

8. Severe Allergic Reactions: If you develop swelling, hives, or difficulty breathing after exposure to an allergen, seek immediate medical care. This could indicate anaphylaxis, a life-threatening condition.

Knowing when to seek help is an essential part of taking care of yourself. Don't hesitate to reach out to a healthcare provider if you're ever unsure about your symptoms. It's always better to be safe and get professional advice to keep your health on track during your college years.

EXAMPLE SCENARIOS FOR TEENAGERS

- **Unusual Chest Pain:** If you ever experience unexpected chest pain or tightness after physical activity or even at rest, don't ignore it. While it could be something minor, chest pain can sometimes signal a more serious issue. Take a moment to assess how you're feeling, and if the pain persists or worsens, call campus health services or visit the nearest urgent care. It's always better to be cautious when dealing with any unusual symptoms.
- **Severe Stomach Pain Before Class:** Imagine you wake up with intense stomach pain that doesn't go away after a few hours. If the pain worsens or you notice symptoms like vomiting or a high fever, it's important to skip class and seek

medical help right away to rule out more serious issues like appendicitis.

4. CPR and Stroke Awareness: Saving Lives on Campus

Learning CPR (Cardiopulmonary Resuscitation) and recognizing the signs of a stroke are crucial life-saving skills for everyone, including teenagers. In emergencies, these abilities can make a significant difference before professional help arrives.

A stroke happens when the blood supply to part of the brain is interrupted. Recognizing the signs quickly can mean the difference between recovery and permanent damage. Use the acronym **BEFAST** to spot stroke symptoms:

- **Balance**: Is there sudden difficulty with balance or coordination?
- **Eyes**: Has there been a sudden change in vision or trouble seeing out of one or both eyes?
- **Face Drooping**: Ask the person to smile. Does one side of the face droop?
- **Arm Weakness**: Ask them to raise both arms. Does one arm drift downward?
- **Speech Difficulty**: Can they repeat a simple sentence? Is their speech slurred or strange?
- **Time**: If any of these symptoms are present, call 911 immediately and note when the symptoms first appeared.

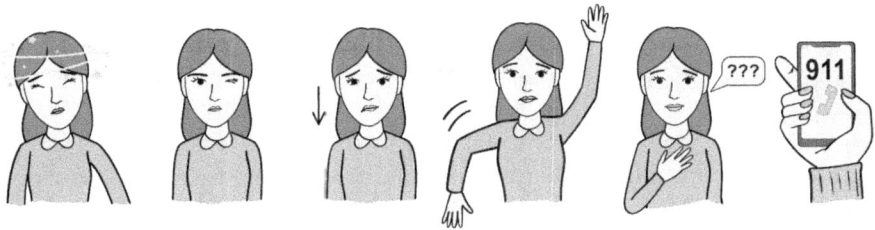

BEFAST: Balance, Eyes, Face, Arms, Speech, Time.

CPR is used when someone's breathing or heartbeat has stopped, such as in cases of cardiac arrest or drowning. It's a skill you hope to never use but should be ready for. **Hands-Only CPR** is recommended for untrained bystanders or when you're unsure of conventional CPR techniques. Here's how to perform it:

1. Check Responsiveness: Tap the person gently and shout. If there's no response, call for help immediately. If you're not alone, have someone else call 911 while you start CPR.

2. Open the Airway: Tilt the person's head back and lift their chin to open their airway.

3. Check for Breathing: Look, listen, and feel for breathing for no more than ten seconds. Occasional gasping doesn't count as normal breathing.

4. Give Chest Compressions: Place the heel of one hand in the center of their chest, with the other hand on top, interlocking your fingers. Keeping your arms straight, press down at least two inches (five centimeters) deep. Perform compressions at a rate of 100-120 per minute, matching the rhythm of "Stayin' Alive" by the Bee Gees.

5. Continue Compressions: After thirty compressions, give two rescue breaths, and continue this cycle. To give rescue breaths, tilt the person's head back, lift their chin, and pinch their nose shut to open the airway. Take a deep breath, seal your mouth over theirs, and blow for about one second, watching for their chest to rise. After the chest falls, give a second breath and continue if needed. Do not stop until emergency help arrives or the person shows signs of life.

6. Use an AED: If an Automated External Defibrillator (AED) is available, use it immediately by following its voice instructions. If not, continue CPR until help arrives.

Knowing these skills can help save a life in a critical moment, providing essential care until professionals take over.

 **1** Call 911 or ask someone else to

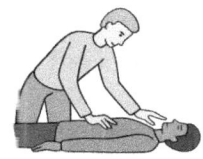 **2** Lay the person on their back and open their airways

 **3** If they are not breathing, start CPR

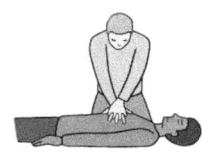 **4** Thirty chest compressions

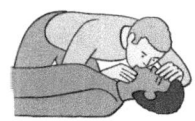 **5** Two rescue breaths

 **6** Repeat untill an ambulance or AED arrives

Example Scenarios for Teenagers

- **Responding to a Cardiac Emergency:** Imagine you're at the gym and someone collapses suddenly. If they aren't breathing and have no pulse, knowing CPR could save their life. Begin chest compressions immediately while someone else calls for emergency help. CPR can make a critical difference in those precious minutes before professional help can arrive.
- **Recognizing Stroke Symptoms in a Friend:** You're hanging out with a friend when they suddenly struggle to speak and their face starts drooping on one side. Recognizing these signs of a stroke (FAST: Face drooping, Arm weakness, Speech difficulties, Time to call 911) could help you act quickly, potentially saving their life by getting them medical attention right away.

4. Emotional Management and Mental Health

Managing your emotions and mental health is just as important as taking care of your physical well-being, especially during the ups and downs of college life. In this chapter, you'll explore the importance of recognizing and accepting your emotions, and learn practical strategies for coping with stress and anxiety. From practicing gratitude through journaling to building a strong support system with friends, family, and counselors, this chapter provides tools for maintaining emotional balance. You'll also discover ways to navigate difficult emotions, including grief and loss, and how to seek help when needed. With the right support and techniques, you can build resilience and thrive emotionally throughout your college journey.

1. Identifying, Understanding, and Accepting Your Emotions

Effective emotional management starts with recognizing and understanding your feelings. It's not just about controlling emotions but also understanding why they happen and how they affect your behavior.

Emotions are complex and can strongly influence your thoughts and actions. Accurately naming and understanding them is essential for managing them. Expanding your emotional vocabulary beyond basics like sadness, anger, joy, and frustration helps you express yourself more precisely. For example, knowing the difference between being "disappointed" (unmet expectations) and "disheartened" (loss of hope) can give you greater insight into your emotional state.

Some emotions are straightforward, while others are more complex, combining elements of basic emotions. Nostalgia, for instance, mixes happiness and sadness, while jealousy combines anger, fear, and sadness. Situations can trigger specific emotions, such as anxiety before an exam or joy before a trip. Emotions also arise in relationships, like empathy, envy, or gratitude, affecting how you interact with others.

Using an Emotion Chart

An emotion chart or wheel can help you distinguish between similar feelings and understand your emotional experiences more clearly. For example:

- **Annoyed vs. Furious**: Annoyance is mild irritation, while fury is intense anger that might need physical exercise or deep breathing to manage.
- **Apprehensive vs. Terrified**: Apprehension is mild unease, while terror is a strong fear that may require more significant coping strategies.
- **Content vs. Elated**: Contentment is gentle satisfaction, while elation is a high-energy joy that you might want to share with others.

You can use an emotion chart in different ways:

1. Regular Check-ins: Get into the habit of checking in with your emotions throughout the day to become more attuned to your feelings.

2. During Stress or Conflict: When feeling stressed, pause and consult the emotion chart to clarify your feelings before acting.

3. Enhance Communication: Using specific terms from the chart improves communication, making it easier for others to understand your perspective.

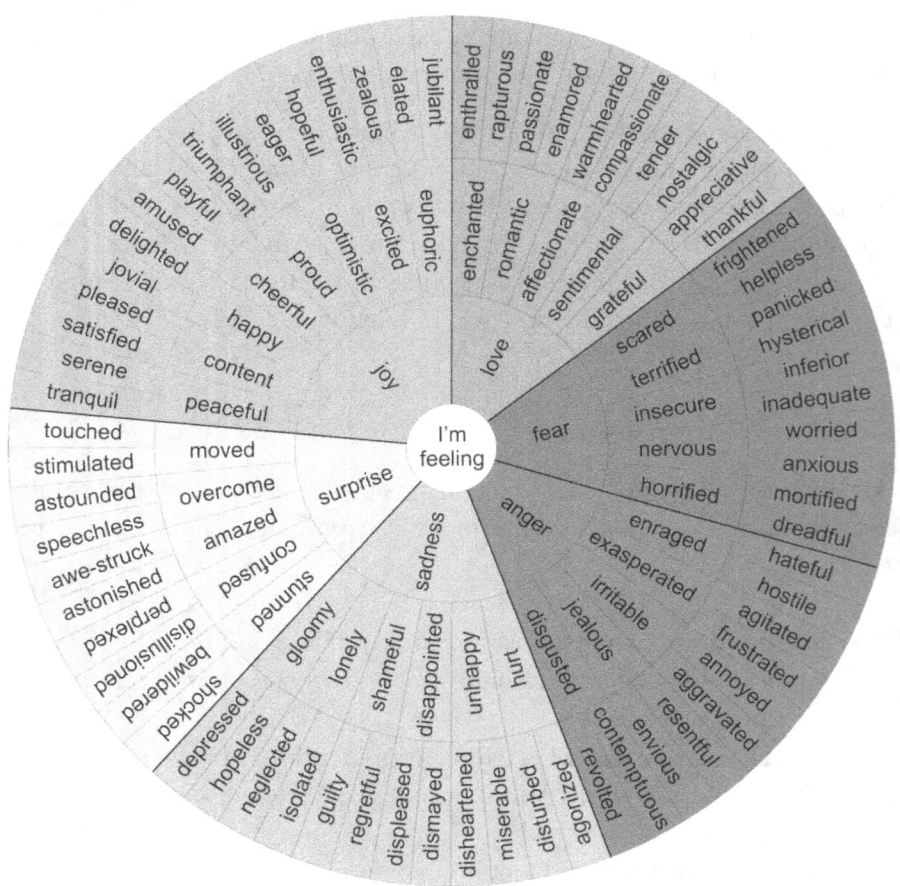

Techniques for Identifying Emotions

1. Physical Clues: Your body often shows signs before you can name your emotions. A racing heart might indicate anxiety, while a heavy chest might suggest sadness.

2. Behavioral Observations: Notice how your emotions affect your behavior. Are you withdrawing from friends when sad or becoming more sarcastic when irritated?

3. Journaling: Writing about your daily experiences can reveal patterns in your emotional responses.

The Importance of Acknowledging Emotions

Accepting your emotions is crucial for self-compassion and mental health. Acknowledging your feelings allows you to process and manage them more effectively. It also improves communication with others, helping you express your emotions clearly and fostering healthy relationships.

Applying Emotional Awareness

Managing emotions in practice might involve taking a deep breath when anger flares, or sharing good news with a friend to amplify your joy. These skills are foundational for emotional intelligence and are essential for responding constructively to your feelings.

Accepting your Emotions

Emotional acceptance is a key step in managing emotions. It involves acknowledging and embracing your feelings without judgment, whether they are positive or negative. This acceptance helps you process emotions in a healthy way, promoting mental well-being.

Recognizing that emotions are a natural part of being human allows you to see their value. For instance, sadness can highlight what matters to you, fear can warn of potential threats, and happiness shows your needs are being met.

The benefits of accepting your emotions include:

- **Reduced Emotional Distress**: Accepting your emotions reduces the stress that comes from resisting them, leading to a more balanced state.
- **Improved Mental Health**: Emotional acceptance is linked to lower rates of anxiety and depression.
- **Enhanced Self-Awareness**: Accepting your emotions promotes greater understanding of yourself, which can improve decision-making and relationships.

Practical Steps for Accepting your Emotions

1. Identify and Name Your Emotions: Use tools like an emotion chart to identify and articulate what you're feeling.

2. Allow Yourself to Feel: Give yourself permission to fully experience your emotions without trying to change them.

3. Reflect on the Purpose of Emotions: Consider what each emotion is telling you. Anger, for example, might signal a need to address a sense of injustice.

4. Practice Mindfulness: Mindfulness techniques, like deep breathing or meditation, help you observe emotions without judgment, keeping you grounded.

5. Seek Support if Needed: If emotions feel overwhelming, seek support from friends, family, or professionals who can help you process your feelings.

6. Normalize Emotional Experiences: Sharing your emotions with others helps normalize your experiences and fosters connections with those who may feel similarly.

Accepting your emotions creates a foundation for emotional health and personal growth. By recognizing your feelings and their significance, you take important steps toward better emotional management and well-being.

EXAMPLE SCENARIOS FOR TEENAGERS

- **Dealing with Homesickness:** During your first few weeks of college, it's normal to feel a bit overwhelmed or lonely as you adjust to being away from home. Instead of ignoring these emotions, take time to recognize what you're feeling. Journaling or talking to someone about your experience can help you process homesickness and understand that these emotions are a natural part of transitioning to a new environment.
- **Handling Frustration with Academics:** If you find yourself feeling frustrated or stressed about your coursework, try to identify the root cause of your emotions. Are you struggling with time management, or do you feel unprepared for the material? By understanding your emotions, you can accept them without judgment and take proactive steps – like reaching out to a professor or creating a study plan – to improve the situation.

2. Stress and Anxiety: Coping Mechanisms for College Life

Stress can show up in many forms and can be triggered by things like school deadlines, social pressures, changes in relationships, or extracurricular commitments. Recognizing early signs of stress, such as irritability, changes in sleep, or decreased motivation, is key to managing it before it becomes overwhelming. Here are some practical ways to cope with stress:

1. Identify the Sources of Stress: Keep a journal to track what causes you stress and how you react. Understanding your triggers helps you prepare for future situations.

2. Develop Healthy Habits: Regular physical activity, a balanced diet, and adequate sleep are essential for reducing stress. Exercise, in particular, can improve your mood and reduce anxiety.

3. Learn Relaxation Techniques: Practices like deep breathing, meditation, or yoga can calm your mind and body, helping you gain a new perspective on stressful situations.

4. Set Realistic Goals: Break tasks into smaller steps and set achievable goals. This can prevent feelings of being overwhelmed and make your tasks feel more manageable.

5. Prioritize Your Tasks: Use to-do lists or planners to organize your time. Knowing what needs to be done and when can reduce the anxiety of tight schedules and deadlines.

6. Maintain Social Connections: Talk about your stress with friends, family, or counselors for emotional support and different perspectives. Social support is powerful in managing stress.

7. Take Time for Yourself: Make time for activities you enjoy, whether it's reading, playing video games, or simply relaxing. Leisure activities are essential for your mental health.

MEDITATION

Meditation involves focusing your attention to achieve a calm and stable state of mind. There are different types, like mindfulness meditation, guided meditation, and transcendental meditation, all aiming to promote mental peace and emotional resilience. Here are some benefits:

- **Reduces Stress and Anxiety**: Regular meditation promotes relaxation and helps you better manage stress.
- **Improves Concentration**: Meditation can strengthen your attention span, which is helpful for academic performance.
- **Enhances Emotional Health**: It encourages a more positive outlook, greater self-awareness, and improved social interactions.
- **Promotes Better Sleep**: Meditation calms your mind before bed, making it easier to fall and stay asleep.

Here's how to start practicing meditation:

1. Find a Quiet Space: Choose a peaceful spot where you won't be disturbed, whether it's a corner of your room or a quiet park.

2. Set a Regular Time: Consistency is important. Try to meditate at the same time each day, whether in the morning or before bed.

3. Use Guided Meditations: If you're new to meditation, guided sessions can help. Apps like Headspace or Waking Up offer step-by-step instructions.

4. Focus on Your Breath: One simple form of meditation is focusing on your breath. Breathe naturally and pay attention to the sensation of your breath. When your mind wanders, gently bring your attention back to your breath. This process strengthens your ability to focus and stay present. Over time, you'll catch wandering thoughts sooner, but remember that some days will be easier than others. Approach meditation with patience and kindness toward yourself. Each time you bring your focus back to your breath, you're strengthening your mindfulness.

5. Start with Short Sessions: Begin with just three minutes a day, and gradually increase to ten minutes as you get more comfortable. It's better to meditate for a few minutes daily than to do longer sessions infrequently.

6. Explore Different Techniques: Over time, try different techniques to see what works best for you. Some might prefer focusing on a mantra, while others enjoy mindfulness or walking meditation.

Incorporating meditation into your daily routine can bring significant benefits for both your mental and emotional health. It's a practical tool that not only helps manage stress but also improves mental focus, emotional stability, and overall well-being.

Example Scenarios for Teenagers

- **Overwhelming Deadlines:** When multiple assignments and exams are piling up, it's easy to feel stressed. Instead of letting anxiety take over, break your tasks into smaller, manageable steps. Use tools like to-do lists or a planner to organize your time effectively. Taking breaks between study sessions and going on short walks can also help reduce stress and keep you focused.
- **Using Meditation Before a Big Exam:** Imagine it's the night before a major exam, and you're feeling overwhelmed. Instead of spiraling into panic mode, take five minutes to sit quietly, close your eyes, and focus on your breathing. This simple meditation can calm your mind and help you feel more centered and ready.

3. Journaling: A Simple Tool for Gratitude

Gratitude journaling involves writing down things you're grateful for, shifting your focus from what's missing or negative to what's positive in your life. This practice helps you appreciate everyday experiences and relationships that are often taken for granted. Here are some key benefits of gratitude journaling:

- **Enhances Positivity**: Regularly focusing on the good in your life increases overall happiness and well-being.
- **Reduces Stress**: Gratitude journaling offers a healthier perspective, countering the tunnel vision stress and anxiety can create.
- **Improves Sleep**: Writing in your journal before bed can calm your mind, promoting better sleep.
- **Strengthens Relationships**: Reflecting on and expressing gratitude for others can enhance your connections and increase empathy.

Here's how to start a gratitude journal:

1. Choose Your Medium: Whether it's a physical journal, a digital app, or a notepad, pick what you enjoy using. Consistency is key.

2. Set a Routine: Write at the same time each day, like in the morning to start positively or in the evening to reflect on the day.

3. Keep It Simple: Start by listing three things you're grateful for daily, or just one thing without repeating it, which helps you notice new blessings.

4. Be Specific: Instead of general statements like "I'm thankful for my family," try "I'm thankful my sister called today to check in."

5. Reflect Deeply: Occasionally, write more about a person or experience you're grateful for, describing how it impacted you.

6. Review Regularly: Reread your past entries on tough days to remind yourself of the good in your life.

Gratitude journaling is a powerful tool that can transform your mindset, making you more joyful and fulfilled. By regularly practicing gratitude, you train your mind to notice positives, fostering resilience and boosting your emotional health.

EXAMPLE SCENARIOS FOR TEENAGERS

- **Dealing with a Tough Day:** After a challenging day filled with academic pressure or personal struggles, it's easy to feel overwhelmed. In these moments, grab your journal and write down three things you're grateful for, no matter how small. Whether it's a kind text from a friend, a good meal, or simply getting through the day, this practice can shift your focus to the positives and help reduce stress.
- **Feeling Stuck or Unmotivated:** If you're feeling unmotivated or stuck in a rut, journaling about moments that have made you happy or proud in the past can reignite a sense of gratitude. Reflecting on the good things in your life, no

matter how big or small, helps create a more positive mindset and fosters a sense of appreciation, even on tough days.

4. Building a Support System: Friends, Family, and Counselors

Transitioning to college life can be exciting, but it also comes with challenges. Whether you're navigating academic stress, homesickness, or personal issues, building a strong support system is key to maintaining your mental and emotional health. Surrounding yourself with people who care about your well-being can make all the difference as you adjust to this new chapter in your life.

Your support system may include friends, family, and counselors, each offering unique perspectives and strengths.

1. Friends: One of the first places to look for support in college is among your peers. Developing friendships with classmates, roommates, and others on campus can provide a sense of belonging. Friends often share similar experiences and can relate to what you're going through. Whether you're having a tough day or just need someone to talk to, a trusted friend can be a great source of comfort and understanding.

2. Family: While you may be away from home, your family can still be a crucial part of your support network. Staying connected with family members, whether through phone calls, texts, or visits, can help you feel grounded. They know you best and can provide perspective, encouragement, and advice when you need it most. Don't hesitate to lean on your family when college life feels overwhelming.

3. Counselors: College counseling services offer a professional resource for students who need extra emotional or mental health support. Talking to a counselor can help you work through feelings of anxiety, depression, or any other challenges that arise. They're trained to listen without judgment and offer coping strategies tailored to your situation. Counseling services are confidential and can be an essential part of your support system when you're facing difficult situations.

TIPS FOR BUILDING A SUPPORT SYSTEM:

1. Reach Out: It's important to take the initiative to connect with others. Join clubs, attend campus events, or simply introduce yourself to classmates. Building friendships takes time, but making an effort will help you form lasting connections.

2. Stay in Touch: Keep communication open with your family, even if you're far away. Regular check-ins can provide emotional stability and remind you that you're not alone.

3. Use Campus Resources: Don't be afraid to seek help from college counseling services. They're there to support you, and many students find it helpful to talk to a professional during stressful periods.

4. Be Honest About Your Needs: It's okay to express when you need support, whether to friends, family, or counselors. Letting people know what you're going through will help them provide the right kind of help.

A strong support system can help you navigate the ups and downs of college life, keeping you balanced, healthy, and emotionally secure.

EXAMPLE SCENARIOS FOR TEENAGERS

- **Reaching Out to Friends:** After a stressful exam, you feel overwhelmed. Instead of keeping it to yourself, you text a close friend to grab coffee and talk. Sharing your feelings with someone you trust helps ease the burden, and your friend's support reminds you that you're not facing college stress alone.
- **Leaning on Family:** Homesickness hits after a tough week, so you call your family. Hearing their familiar voices and chatting about your day brings comfort. They remind you it's okay to feel this way and offer encouraging advice. Having family to lean on helps you feel grounded and supported, even from afar.

5. Grief and Loss: How to Navigate Emotional Challenges

Experiencing loss is a natural part of life, but learning how to cope with grief is essential for emotional resilience. This section provides strategies to help teenagers understand and manage their feelings of loss, whether it's the death of a loved one, the end of a friendship, or another significant life change. Understanding these emotions and having tools to cope can help with healing and personal growth.

Understanding Grief

- **Recognize the Stages of Grief**: Grief is a deeply personal process that often unfolds in stages. You may first experience *denial*, where the loss feels too overwhelming to accept. Then, you might feel *anger*, either at the situation or even at yourself or others. In the *bargaining* stage, you might find yourself thinking about "what if" scenarios, hoping things could have gone differently. After that, *depression* can set in, where feelings of sadness and loss weigh heavily. Finally, with time, many reach *acceptance*, where they start to come to terms with the loss. Understanding that these stages are normal and may not happen in order can help you feel less overwhelmed by your emotions.
- **Allow Yourself to Feel**: Grief brings a flood of emotions, and it's important to give yourself permission to feel them fully. You may experience sadness, frustration, guilt, or even moments of relief. Whatever you feel is valid. Avoiding or suppressing these emotions might seem easier, but it can slow down the healing process. By allowing yourself to grieve, you're giving your heart and mind the space they need to heal.

EFFECTIVE COPING STRATEGIES

1. Talk About It: Sharing your feelings with someone you trust, like a friend, family member, or counselor, can be healing.

2. Maintain Routines: Keeping regular routines can offer a sense of stability during emotional challenges.

3. Take Care of Your Physical Health: Your physical well-being impacts your emotional health. Be mindful of sleep, nutrition, and exercise.

4. Seek Professional Help: If grief feels overwhelming, talking to a mental health professional can offer significant support.

ENGAGE IN MEANINGFUL ACTIVITIES

1. Honor the Memory: Engaging in activities like creating a scrapbook or participating in a charity event can help you honor what you've lost.

2. Find Creative Outlets: Expressing yourself through art, writing, or music can provide a therapeutic release for your emotions.

NAVIGATING THROUGH LOSS

1. Give Yourself Time: Grieving is personal, and everyone's process is different. Allow yourself time without feeling pressured to move on quickly.

2. Recognize Growth: Over time, try to acknowledge how you've grown from the experience, finding new strength and appreciation for life.

Grieving is a deeply personal journey, and there's no right or wrong way to navigate it. By giving yourself the space to feel, seeking support when needed, and finding meaningful ways to honor your loss, you can gradually find healing and growth. Over time, you may discover new strength, resilience, and a greater appreciation for life's precious moments, allowing you to move forward while still cherishing the memories of what was lost.

Example Scenarios for Teenagers

- **Losing a Loved One:** After hearing about the passing of a relative, you feel numb and disconnected from everything. Instead of isolating yourself, you confide in a close friend. Talking about your emotions and reminiscing about good memories helps you process the grief and feel a sense of comfort during this tough time.
- **Seeking Support:** Struggling to focus on schoolwork after a loss, you reach out to a campus counselor. The counselor listens and offers coping strategies, like journaling or mindfulness. This professional support helps you understand that grieving takes time and gives you tools to navigate the emotions while still managing your daily responsibilities.

5. Managing College Relationships

Building and maintaining healthy relationships is a key part of the college experience. From navigating life with a new roommate to forming lasting friendships and staying connected with family, relationships play a vital role in your well-being and personal growth. In this chapter, you'll learn strategies for resolving conflicts and creating harmony with roommates, while also exploring the positive impact friendships can have on your mental health. Additionally, you'll find tips on how to maintain strong ties with family, even when you're far from home. Whether you're making new connections or nurturing existing ones, this chapter will guide you in creating meaningful relationships that support your overall wellness in college.

1. Roommate Harmony: Conflict Resolution

Living with a roommate is often one of the most exciting yet challenging parts of college life. Sharing a space with someone, especially if it's your first time living away from home, can be a great opportunity to build friendships and learn valuable communication skills. However, it's natural for conflicts to arise when two people with different habits, personalities, and routines are living together. The key to maintaining roommate harmony is learning how to navigate these conflicts calmly and respectfully.

Conflict doesn't have to ruin your relationship with your roommate – in fact, handling disagreements well can strengthen your bond. By practicing good communication and showing mutual respect, you can turn your shared living experience into a positive one.

Tips for Resolving Roommate Conflicts:

1. Communicate Openly: The first step in preventing or resolving conflict is clear communication. Talk with your roommate about your needs, preferences, and boundaries early on, whether it's about quiet hours, sharing food, or cleaning responsibilities. Don't wait until a small annoyance turns into a major issue – regular, honest conversations can prevent misunderstandings.

2. Listen Actively: When conflicts arise, it's essential to listen to your roommate's perspective. Try to understand their point of view before reacting. This doesn't mean you have to agree with them, but showing empathy and patience can help you both find common ground.

3. Set Boundaries: Everyone has different preferences when it comes to shared spaces. To avoid future misunderstandings, discuss boundaries early in the relationship. For example, you might want to set rules about borrowing each other's belongings, having guests over, or managing noise levels. These boundaries help establish respect and prevent future tension.

4. Stay Calm During Disagreements: If a conflict occurs, try to remain calm and avoid letting emotions escalate the situation. Approaching the issue with a cool head allows you to focus on finding solutions rather than making the problem worse.

5. Find Compromises: Resolving conflict often involves meeting in the middle. Be willing to compromise and find solutions that work for both you and your roommate. For example, if one of you is a night owl and the other an early riser, you might agree on quiet hours during certain times.

6. Involve a Mediator if Needed: If you and your roommate can't reach an agreement, it may help to involve a neutral third party, such as a Resident Assistant (RA). An RA can mediate the discussion and offer fair solutions based on their experience working with students.

Learning to resolve conflicts effectively with your roommate is a valuable skill that will serve you throughout your college experience – and beyond. With open communication, respect, and a little flexibility, you can maintain a positive and harmonious living environment.

EXAMPLE SCENARIOS FOR TEENAGERS

- **Disagreements Over Cleanliness:** If you and your roommate have different standards of cleanliness, it's important to have an open conversation early on. Instead of letting frustration build, calmly explain your expectations and listen to their perspective as well. You might find a middle ground, like creating a cleaning schedule that works for both of you. Respectful communication is key to preventing bigger issues down the road.
- **Noise and Study Time:** If your roommate often plays loud music while you're trying to study, it can create tension. Approach them kindly, explaining how the noise impacts your ability to focus. Together, you can come up with solutions, like using headphones or setting designated quiet hours. Finding

compromises helps maintain a peaceful living environment and strengthens your relationship.

2. Socializing and MentalHealth: The Power of Friendships

College is an exciting time filled with new experiences, and one of the most important aspects of this journey is forming and maintaining friendships. Friendships during this period are not only a source of joy and companionship, but they also play a crucial role in supporting your mental health. Having friends you can rely on during the ups and downs of college life helps build resilience, increase feelings of belonging, and even improve self-confidence. Socializing in a healthy, balanced way can provide emotional support that makes a big difference in your overall well-being.

However, building lasting friendships takes effort and understanding. College life is busy, and it can be easy to feel isolated, especially in a new environment. But with a little intentionality, you can cultivate meaningful connections that will support you throughout your college years.

Tips for Building and Maintaining Friendships:

1. Be Open and Approachable: Friendships start with small gestures. Smile, make eye contact, and be approachable in social settings. This creates an inviting atmosphere, making it easier for others to initiate conversations with you.

2. Listen Actively: Good friends pay attention to each other. Practice active listening by focusing on what your friend is saying, asking questions, and showing genuine interest. This will make your friends feel valued and understood.

3. Show Empathy: College can be challenging, and your friends will need emotional support just as much as you do. Try to understand their feelings and offer a listening ear or a kind word when they're going through tough times.

4. Be Reliable and Trustworthy: Trust is the foundation of strong friendships. Show up when you say you will, keep your promises, and offer a shoulder to lean on. Being dependable helps strengthen bonds.

5. Celebrate and Support Each Other: A good friend is there for both the highs and lows. Celebrate your friends' achievements, whether it's an academic success or a personal win. Likewise, be there to comfort and support them during tough times.

6. Make Time for Your Friends: Between classes, studying, and extracurriculars, time can slip away quickly. Make an effort to regularly connect with friends, whether it's grabbing coffee or catching up over a call.

Building strong friendships in college can enhance your emotional health and create a support system that makes the challenges of college life more manageable. By being open, empathetic, and reliable, you can nurture friendships that will not only help you during college but last a lifetime.

EXAMPLE SCENARIOS FOR TEENAGERS

- **Feeling Isolated:** If you find yourself feeling lonely or disconnected in college, remember that building friendships takes time. Start by joining clubs or activities that align with your interests. Initiating small conversations with classmates or attending social events can help you meet people with similar hobbies, which can ultimately provide you with a sense of belonging.
- **Finding Balance:** After weeks of focusing solely on classes, you notice you're feeling drained and lonely. You decide to meet up with friends for a movie night. Spending time together helps you unwind, laugh, and feel more connected, reminding you that friendships are essential for emotional well-being.

3. Family Ties: Maintaining Connections While Away

Feeling homesick or missing your friends and family is a common experience, especially if you're away from home for the first time or if your friends have moved away. Such feelings can be intense and impact your emotional well-being. Missing your loved ones can trigger feelings of loneliness, sadness, or even anxiety. It's important to recognize these emotions as normal responses to separation from those you care about, but it's also important to focus on building a new community where you are. Reaching out to new friends, joining clubs, or staying connected with people from home can help you feel more grounded and supported.

Here are some practical steps for coping with homesickness:

1. Stay Connected: Make regular communication a priority. Utilize technology – such as social media, texting, video calls – to keep in touch. Scheduled calls or video chats can give you something to look forward to and help bridge the gap.

2. Create a Support Network: Build a new support network in your current location. While this doesn't replace your loved ones, having friends and acquaintances nearby can provide emotional support and reduce feelings of isolation.

3. Share Your Feelings: Don't hesitate to share how you're feeling with others, whether it's with friends who are physically close or those far away. Often, they might be feeling the same way, and sharing can be mutually comforting.

4. Keep Mementos: Keep photos or personal items that remind you of your loved ones close by. These can serve as comforting reminders of your connections and the good times you've shared.

5. Stay Active: Engage in activities that keep your mind occupied. Join clubs, volunteer, or participate in local events. Staying active can help you make new friends and reduce the feelings of missing home.

6. Plan Visits: If possible, plan visits home or arrange for friends and family to visit you. Having these visits to look forward to can significantly alleviate feelings of sadness and homesickness.

7. Establish New Traditions: Create new traditions in your current environment. This can help make your new location feel more like home and can give you a sense of belonging and community.

EXAMPLE SCENARIOS FOR TEENAGERS

- **Staying Connected:** During a busy week of exams, you suddenly miss home. You decide to video call your family, and hearing their voices instantly lifts your mood. Staying in touch, even with a quick text or call, can help maintain strong family bonds while easing the transition to college life. Remember: homesickness is normal, especially during the first few months, and maintaining communication can ease that feeling.
- **Sharing Milestones:** After acing a tough class, you text your family to share the good news. They celebrate your success, even from afar, making you feel supported. Regularly updating your family on big or small moments helps you feel connected and reminds you that they're cheering you on from home.

6. Digital Health and Well-being

In today's digital world, managing your online life is just as important as taking care of your physical and mental health. From social media to late-night study sessions, screen time can easily become overwhelming, affecting everything from your sleep to your self-esteem. In this chapter, I'll go over the impact of digital habits on your well-being and provide strategies for creating healthy boundaries with technology. You'll learn how to balance screen time, manage the effects of social media on your mental health, and even discover the benefits of taking a digital detox. With these tools, you can maintain a positive relationship with technology while keeping your health a priority.

1. Screen Time and Sleep: Setting Healthy Boundaries

Starting college brings many exciting opportunities and challenges, but it also introduces new stressors that can affect your mental and physical health. One key area to focus on is balancing screen time, especially in terms of social media and digital communication, with getting enough sleep. Good sleep is essential for emotional well-being, academic performance, and overall health. However, excessive screen use – especially before bed – can interfere with sleep patterns and contribute to feelings of exhaustion and overwhelm.

Many college students find themselves glued to their phones, laptops, or tablets late into the night, which can impact both the quality and duration of sleep. The blue light emitted by screens can disrupt melatonin production, a hormone that helps regulate your sleep-wake cycle, making it harder to fall asleep and stay asleep. On top of that, constant notifications, social media scrolling, and fear of missing out (FOMO) can keep your mind overstimulated when you should be winding down.

Here are some tips for setting healthy boundaries between screen time and sleep:

1. Create a "Screen-Free" Bedtime Routine: Develop a habit of putting away all devices at least thirty to sixty minutes before you plan to go to sleep. Instead of browsing online or scrolling through social media, spend this time reading a book, practicing mindfulness, or listening to calming music. A screen-free routine can signal your brain that it's time to rest, helping you fall asleep more easily.

2. Set a Sleep Schedule: Try to go to bed and wake up at the same time each day, even on weekends. Consistency in your sleep schedule helps regulate your body's internal clock, making it easier to fall asleep and wake up feeling refreshed. If you're mindful about when you go to bed, you're more likely to naturally reduce late-night screen usage.

3. Use Night Mode or Blue Light Filters: If you have to use your phone or laptop in the evening, turn on night mode or use a blue light filter. Many devices come with this option, which reduces the impact of blue light on your sleep. However, this shouldn't be a substitute for reducing overall screen time before bed.

4. Disable Notifications: Constant notifications can keep you tethered to your phone or laptop, even when you're trying to wind down for the night. Turn off notifications from social media and other non-essential apps during your designated screen-free time or use the "Do Not Disturb" feature.

5. Keep Devices Out of Reach: Charge your phone away from your bed or in another room altogether. This reduces the temptation to check it every time you wake up during the night or just before bed.

By setting these boundaries, you're not only protecting your sleep but also promoting better mental health. A good night's rest can help reduce stress, improve focus, and boost your mood, making it easier to tackle the challenges of college life. Remember, balance is key – use your devices wisely, but don't let them interfere with the rest your body and mind need to thrive.

EXAMPLE SCENARIOS FOR TEENAGERS

- **Night-Time Phone Habit:** You're scrolling through social media in bed, but it's actually already midnight, and you have an 8 am class the next day. Upon realizing that you're not getting enough sleep, set a "no phone" rule an hour before bed. This small change helps you wind down and get better rest for the next day.
- **Balancing Schoolwork and Screen Time:** If schoolwork on your laptop is keeping you up late, set a schedule that includes breaks away from screens throughout the day. You could use apps like Forest or Freedom that remind you to take breaks or block social media during study sessions.

2. Social Media: Navigating the Impact on Self-Esteem

Social media has revolutionized how we communicate, providing a space to connect, share experiences, and access information. However, its impact on self-esteem can be profound, especially for teenagers. The constant exposure to idealized images and lifestyles can lead to unrealistic comparisons, leaving many feeling inadequate or insecure. When we scroll through curated highlights of others' lives, it's easy to believe that everyone else is happier, more successful, or more attractive. This skewed perception often results in lower self-esteem, as we compare our behind-the-scenes moments to others' carefully crafted online personas.

The link between social media and self-esteem is complex. On the one hand, platforms can offer validation through likes, comments, and shares, providing a quick boost in confidence. However, this validation can become addictive, making individuals overly reliant on external approval. When that validation doesn't come, feelings of rejection or self-doubt can arise. Additionally, cyberbullying, negative comments, and exclusion from online groups can further damage one's self-worth.

To maintain a healthy relationship with social media, it's essential to adopt strategies that protect your self-esteem while still enjoying the benefits of online interaction.

Strategies for Safe Social Media Use

1. Set Time Limits: Limiting time spent on social media can reduce the impact it has on self-esteem. The American Academy of Pediatrics suggests no more than one to two hours of screen time per day for entertainment purposes, ensuring this time doesn't interfere with sleep, physical activity, or responsibilities.

2. Be Critical of What You See: Remember that what people post online is often a highlight reel, not their complete reality. Being mindful of this can prevent negative comparisons.

3. Use Privacy Settings: Control who can see your posts and personal information. Protecting your privacy can reduce unwanted stress and ensure a safer online experience.

4. Engage Positively: Focus on spreading positivity and supporting others. Avoid negative interactions that can cause unnecessary conflict or stress.

5. Educate Yourself: Stay informed about social media trends and potential risks. Share this knowledge with friends and family to help them navigate social media safely.

By being mindful of how social media affects your self-esteem and using it responsibly, you can enjoy the positive aspects while protecting your emotional well-being.

EXAMPLE SCENARIOS FOR TEENAGERS

- **Comparing Yourself to Others:** If scrolling through social media leaves you feeling like you don't measure up, it's important to take a step back and remember that people often post highlight reels of their lives, not the full picture. Try limiting the time you spend on these platforms and remind yourself that everyone's journey is different. Focus on your own accomplishments, no matter how small, and surround yourself with positive content that inspires rather than compares.
- **Feeling Left Out:** If you notice a group of friends posting about an event you weren't invited to, it can sting. Rather than dwelling on the exclusion, reach out to a close friend for support or plan something fun together that you enjoy.

3. Digital Detox: Tips for Disconnecting

In today's fast-paced, always-connected world, it can be difficult to imagine stepping away from your phone or computer for even a few hours, let alone a day or more. As you enter college, finding a balance between your digital life and the real world is more important than ever.

Social media, though fun and convenient, can sometimes contribute to stress, anxiety, and lowered self-esteem, especially when overused. A digital detox – temporarily stepping away from screens and technology – can help you reset and reconnect with the world around you.

The idea of unplugging might seem daunting at first, but it doesn't mean you need to cut yourself off completely. Rather, it's about creating healthier boundaries with your devices and learning to be more intentional with your screen time. Here are some practical tips for disconnecting:

1. Set Daily Limits: Start by setting small, manageable time limits on your daily screen use. You can use app timers to remind you when you've hit your limit for the day. Gradually reducing your time on social media or other digital platforms will help you feel more in control of your tech use without going cold turkey.

2. Designate Tech-Free Zones: Choose specific areas in your dorm room or apartment where screens are off-limits. This might include your bed, dining area, or study space. Keeping tech out of these spaces encourages mindfulness and helps you focus on the present moment, whether you're eating, relaxing, or studying.

3. Schedule Screen-Free Time: Set aside certain times during the day when you disconnect completely. This could be during meals, an hour before bed, or a designated weekend afternoon. Use this time to engage in activities like reading, exercising, or spending time with friends – without the distraction of your phone.

4. Replace Scrolling with Other Activities: Whenever you feel the urge to scroll through social media, try engaging in a different, more fulfilling activity. Whether it's going for a walk, calling a friend, or working on a creative hobby, finding alternatives will help ease the impulse to reach for your phone.

5. Take Social Media Breaks: Consider taking short breaks from social media, such as deactivating your accounts for a weekend or even a week. This can give you space to recharge and refocus, helping you return to your online world with a refreshed perspective and better boundaries.

6. Practice Mindful Tech Use: The goal of a digital detox isn't to completely avoid technology but to use it more mindfully. Before you pick up your phone, ask yourself why you're using it — is it for something necessary or out of habit? Being more conscious of your reasons for using technology can help you create healthier patterns over time.

By taking steps to disconnect and be more intentional with your screen time, you'll find yourself more engaged in your college experience, more connected to the people around you, and more in tune with your own mental health. A digital detox can be a valuable part of self-care, helping you strike the right balance between the virtual world and real life

EXAMPLE SCENARIOS FOR TEENAGERS

- **Weekend Without Social Media:** After feeling overwhelmed by constant notifications, you decide to take a break from social media for the weekend. You turn off your app notifications and spend the time catching up on reading and going for a hike. By Monday, you'll feel more relaxed and refreshed, ready to tackle the week ahead.
- **Study Session Focus:** You notice that every time you sit down to study, your phone becomes a distraction. To stay focused, you put your phone on airplane mode for two hours. Without the temptation to check it, you finish your work faster and you can even reward yourself with some screen time afterward.

7. Balancing Academics and Wellness

Balancing academics with personal well-being is essential for thriving in college. With classes, assignments, and exams demanding your attention, it can be easy to feel overwhelmed. However, managing your time effectively and maintaining a healthy routine can help you stay on track without burning out. In this chapter, I'll explore strategies for managing academic pressures while prioritizing your mental health and well-being. From mastering time management and preventing burnout to using smart study techniques, these tips will help you stay focused, productive, and in control of your college experience. By finding a balance, you can succeed academically while also taking care of yourself.

1. Time Management Skills for Success

Effective time management is a critical skill for college students as they navigate classes, extracurriculars, social life, and personal commitments. Learning to balance these responsibilities can reduce stress, improve academic performance, and enhance overall well-being. Managing your time well helps you stay organized, focused, and in control of your college experience.

Developing strong time management habits takes practice, but it begins with understanding the value of time and identifying the activities that might be holding you back. For example, social media or procrastination (the habit of delaying tasks) can steal time away from important tasks if left unchecked. By learning to manage these distractions and prioritizing your work, you can set yourself up for success.

Tips for Effective Time Management

1. Set Clear Goals: Start by setting specific goals for both the short and long term. These could be daily tasks, like completing an assignment, or longer-term goals, like finishing a project by the end of the semester. Setting clear goals gives you direction and helps you allocate your time effectively.

2. Prioritize Tasks: Focus on the most important tasks first. Ask yourself "What is the one thing I can accomplish today that will make everything else easier?" By tackling high-priority tasks early, you can create momentum and feel more productive throughout the day.

3. Create a Schedule: Planning your day or week in advance is key to staying on track. Use a planner, digital calendar, or time management app to block out study sessions, classes, and free time. Structuring your day this way prevents last-minute stress and ensures you don't miss deadlines.

4. Avoid Multitasking: While it might seem like multitasking helps you get more done, it often reduces your focus and lowers the quality of your work. Instead, concentrate on one task at a time for better results and less mental fatigue.

5. Take Breaks: Regular breaks help maintain your focus and productivity. Try the Pomodoro Technique, where you work for twenty-five-minute intervals followed by a five-minute break. This method can help sustain your concentration and keep you from burning out.

6. Learn to Say No: Sometimes, it's tempting to say yes to every social event or extra commitment. However, learning to say no when necessary is vital for keeping your schedule manageable. Prioritize tasks that align with your goals, and don't be afraid to turn down activities that don't fit.

7. Review and Adjust: Time management is an ongoing process. Regularly review how you're spending your time and make changes as needed. This helps you refine your approach and ensure you're working efficiently.

By following these strategies, you can develop strong time management skills that will help you succeed in college and beyond.

Example Scenarios for Teenagers

- **Balancing Classes and Activities:** You've got a busy week ahead with classes, a club meeting, and a part-time job. To stay on top of things, you use a planner to schedule study time and breaks between activities. By planning ahead, you avoid last-minute stress and still have time to relax in the evenings.
- **Managing Assignments:** If you often wait until the last minute to start assignments, set small, daily goals to tackle work in chunks. For example, if you have a research paper due in two weeks, aim to complete the outline by day three and finish the first draft by day seven. This approach will reduce stress and make managing your workload much easier.

2. Preventing Burnout: Academic Pressure and Mental Health

Preventing burnout in college is essential to maintaining both academic success and mental well-being. College life comes with a lot of responsibilities, and while academic pressure can motivate you to work hard, it can also lead to stress and exhaustion if not managed carefully. Burnout happens when prolonged stress and overwhelming pressure cause mental, emotional, and physical fatigue. Recognizing the signs and taking proactive steps can help you avoid burnout and maintain a healthy balance between academics and self-care.

Understanding Burnout

Burnout can manifest as chronic tiredness, lack of motivation, irritability, or difficulty concentrating. If left unaddressed, it can negatively impact your academic performance, relationships, and overall mental health. It's important to understand that taking care of your mental and emotional health is just as important as succeeding in your studies.

Tips For Understanding Burnout

1. Set Realistic Goals: While it's great to aim high, setting unattainable goals can set you up for frustration. Break large tasks into smaller, manageable steps, and set goals that challenge you without overwhelming you. Celebrate each small achievement to keep yourself motivated.

2. Take Breaks: Pushing through hours of non-stop study might seem productive, but it can actually lead to faster burnout. Make time for breaks throughout your day, whether it's a short walk, a chat with a friend, or time to relax. Stepping away from your work helps recharge your mind.

3. Prioritize Sleep: Lack of sleep is one of the biggest contributors to burnout. While late-night study sessions might feel necessary, getting a good night's rest will improve your focus, mood, and overall well-being. Aim for at least seven to nine hours of sleep each night.

4. Practice Self-Care: Self-care is about nurturing your physical and emotional health. Engage in activities that help you relax and rejuvenate, whether it's exercising, meditating, reading for pleasure, or enjoying time with friends. Making time for self-care can help you maintain your energy and reduce stress.

5. Manage Your Time: Good time management can reduce stress and prevent last-minute panic. Use planners or apps to organize your assignments, exams, and personal commitments. By staying on top of your workload, you can avoid the pressure that comes with procrastination.

6. Reach Out for Help: If you're feeling overwhelmed, don't hesitate to seek support. Talk to a counselor, a trusted professor, or a friend. Sometimes, sharing your feelings and asking for advice can help lighten the load and provide a fresh perspective.

By setting boundaries and taking time to care for yourself, you can protect your mental health and enjoy a more fulfilling, balanced college experience without succumbing to burnout.

EXAMPLE SCENARIOS FOR TEENAGERS

- **Avoiding Overload Before Exams:** You've got three exams next week, and the pressure is building. Instead of cramming all night, create a study schedule that spreads the workload over several days. Make sure you also take short breaks and get enough sleep, to help you stay focused and reduce the risk of burnout.
- **Taking Care of Mental Health:** Mid-semester stress is hitting hard, and you're feeling overwhelmed with assignments. Talk to a trusted friend and set aside some time for yourself to unwind, whether it's going for a walk or practicing mindfulness. Taking these steps will help you recharge and manage the academic pressure more effectively.

3. Studying Smart: Techniques for Focus and Productivity

Studying smart, rather than just studying hard, is key to achieving academic success in college without feeling overwhelmed. Learning how to focus, manage your time effectively, and retain information is essential for balancing your studies with other aspects of college life. Below are some proven techniques and strategies to help you maximize your focus and productivity.

Effective Study Techniques

1. The Pareto Principle (80/20 Rule): The Pareto Principle suggests that 80% of your results come from 20% of your efforts. In terms of studying, this means identifying the most important topics or concepts that will give you the greatest understanding of the subject. Focus your study time on these key areas, rather than spending equal time on everything. This approach helps you study efficiently and retain more critical information.

2. The Pomodoro Technique: This time management method involves breaking your study time into twenty-five-minute focused intervals (called Pomodoros), followed by a five-minute break. After four Pomodoros, take a longer break of fifteen to thirty minutes. This technique helps you maintain focus while avoiding burnout, as it encourages regular rest periods to keep your mind fresh.

3. Spaced Repetition: Instead of cramming all your studying into one long session, spaced repetition is a technique that involves reviewing material at increasing intervals over time. This method strengthens long-term memory retention by revisiting information before you forget it. Tools like flashcards or apps such as Anki can help implement this strategy.

4. Create an Optimal Study Environment: Where you study plays a huge role in how well you focus. Choose a quiet, well-lit space with minimal distractions. Make sure to have all the materials you need at hand to avoid interruptions. Some students find that a little background noise or instrumental music helps them concentrate, but find what works best for you.

5. Efficient Study Planning: Creating a study schedule helps you organize your time and prioritize tasks. Dedicate specific blocks of time to the subjects that require the most attention, and plan around deadlines for assignments and exams. Stick to your schedule, but also allow for flexibility to adapt as needed.

Tips for Boosting Productivity

1. Set Clear Goals for Each Session: At the start of each study session, set specific and measurable goals. For example, instead of "study biology," set a goal to "review chapters four and five and complete the practice questions." This gives you a clear objective and helps you stay focused.

2. Take Breaks: Don't forget to schedule regular breaks. Even short walks or stretching sessions can help reset your mind and increase productivity when you return to studying. Breaks also improve long-term focus and prevent mental fatigue.

3. Use Active Learning Methods: Instead of passively reading textbooks, engage with the material through active learning techniques. This includes summarizing what you've learned, teaching the material to someone else, or applying concepts to real-world scenarios. These methods reinforce your understanding and help with retention.

By incorporating these study techniques into your routine, you'll find it easier to focus, retain information, and manage your time effectively, ultimately making your college experience more productive and less stressful.

Example Scenarios for Teenagers

- **Trouble Staying Focused While Studying:** If you find yourself easily distracted while studying, try using the Pomodoro technique. Set a timer for twenty-five minutes and focus on one task without interruption. When the timer goes off, take a five-minute break. After a few cycles, you'll notice your concentration improving, and you'll be able to retain information more effectively without feeling burnt out.
- **Breaking Down Big Tasks:** Let's say you have a ten-page paper due next week, and it feels overwhelming. Instead of writing it all at once, break it into smaller sections. Dedicate one day for research, another for outlining, and then write a few pages each day. This approach keeps you focused and prevents last-minute stress.

8. Alcohol, Drugs, and Campus Culture

College life often involves navigating new social environments where alcohol, drugs, and peer pressure can play a significant role. Understanding the risks and consequences of substance use is key to making informed decisions that protect your health and well-being. In this chapter, I'll go over how to recognize and respond to these situations responsibly, offering practical strategies for saying no and maintaining your boundaries. Whether you're attending parties or social events, knowing how to handle peer pressure and stay safe will help you enjoy your college experience while staying true to your values. Let's dive into the tools and tips you need to confidently navigate these challenges.

1. Understanding Risks and Consequences

Heading off to college is an exciting time filled with new freedoms, responsibilities, and opportunities. However, this newfound independence also comes with the potential for risks – particularly when it comes to alcohol, drugs, and substance abuse. Understanding these risks and their consequences is essential to making informed choices and protecting your health and well-being during your college years.

While it may be tempting to experiment with alcohol or drugs, especially in social settings, it's important to be aware of the potential dangers. Alcohol and drug use can have immediate effects on your physical and mental health, as well as long-term consequences for your academic success, relationships, and future career. Learning how to navigate these pressures and make responsible decisions can help you avoid many of these pitfalls.

Risks of Alcohol and Substance Abuse

1. Impaired Judgment and Decision-Making: Alcohol and drugs impair your judgment, making it harder to think clearly and make safe choices. This can lead to risky behaviors, such as driving under the influence, unprotected sex, or becoming involved in dangerous situations that you would otherwise avoid.

2. Academic Performance: Frequent alcohol or drug use can affect your academic performance. Impaired concentration, missed classes, and difficulty studying are common consequences, potentially leading to lower grades, academic probation, or even expulsion. Keeping your focus on your academic goals is crucial to college success, and substance use can get in the way of that.

3. Physical and Mental Health: Substance abuse can take a toll on your physical health, leading to hangovers, exhaustion, and more serious medical issues like liver damage or overdose. In addition, alcohol and drugs can worsen mental health problems, such as anxiety and depression, and create dependency, making it difficult to function without using substances.

4. Legal Consequences: Many college students are unaware that underage drinking or using illegal drugs can result in serious legal consequences, such as fines, community service, or a criminal record. Having a legal violation on your record can limit future job prospects and affect your college experience in ways you may not expect.

STRATEGIES FOR STAYING SAFE

1. Know Your Limits: If you choose to drink, do so in moderation. Understand your own limits, and avoid drinking to the point of intoxication. Be mindful of the effects of alcohol and how it impacts your behavior.

2. Set Boundaries: If you are heading to a college party or social event and decide to consume alcohol and drugs, take a moment to set clear limits for yourself. Decide ahead of time how much you'll consume. Having a plan will help you feel less pressured in the moment and will allow you to stay in control of your choices and your safety.

3. Avoid Mixing Substances: Mixing alcohol with drugs, even legal ones like prescription medication, can lead to dangerous and unpredictable reactions. Always be cautious about what you put into your body, and never combine substances.

4. Look Out for Your Friends: Watching out for each other can prevent many harmful situations. If you notice a friend drinking too much or engaging in risky behavior, step in and help them make safer choices.

5. Reach Out for Help: If you're struggling with substance use or feel pressured to use, don't hesitate to seek help. Most colleges offer counseling services, and there are many resources available to support students facing substance abuse challenges.

College is a time of growth and exploration, but it's important to keep your safety and well-being at the forefront. By understanding the risks of alcohol and drugs and making responsible choices, you can protect your health, succeed academically, and enjoy your college experience to the fullest.

Example Scenarios for Teenagers

- **Peer Pressure at a Party:** If you're at a party and feeling pressured to drink alcohol, it's okay to say no. You can simply hold a non-alcoholic drink, like soda or water, and enjoy the event without feeling the need to conform. Having a plan before you go out can help you stay firm in your decisions, especially if friends are trying to convince you otherwise.
- **Curiosity About Drugs:** If you're curious about trying drugs because of things you've seen online or heard from others, take a moment to think about the potential consequences. Understanding the long-term effects on your health, academics, and future opportunities can help you make a more informed decision. It's always a good idea to talk to someone you trust, like a counselor, before making choices that could impact your well-being.

2. Peer Pressure: Strategies for Saying No

Peer pressure is a common experience in college, where new social environments can sometimes make you feel pressured to fit in or participate in activities that don't align with your values. Whether it's alcohol, drugs, or other behaviors, standing your ground and saying "no" is important to maintaining your authenticity and well-being. Learning how to navigate these situations and stay true to yourself can help you manage peer pressure while building healthy, respectful relationships.

It's perfectly normal to want to be accepted and liked by your peers. However, it's equally important to recognize when you're being asked to do something that goes against your beliefs or comfort level. Developing strategies to confidently say "no" in these situations will help you uphold your boundaries and maintain control over your choices.

STRATEGIES FOR SAYING NO TO PEER PRESSURE

1. Know Your Values: Understanding your core values is key to resisting peer pressure. If you're clear about what's important to you – whether it's prioritizing your academics, avoiding substance use, or simply staying true to your personal beliefs – it becomes easier to stand your ground when faced with situations that challenge those values. Ask yourself "Does this action align with who I am or who I want to be?" If the answer is no, it's okay to step away.

2. Use Assertive Communication: It's important to say "no" in a clear and confident manner. Practice assertive communication by using a firm yet polite tone. You can say something like "Thanks for the invite, but I'm not into that," or "I've made a decision to stay sober, and I'm sticking with it." Being direct shows that you're serious about your decision without being confrontational.

3. Offer Alternatives: Sometimes, suggesting an alternative activity can help defuse the situation. For example, if you're invited to a party where you feel pressured to drink, you could suggest doing something else, like catching a movie or hanging out in a more relaxed setting. Offering an alternative shows that you're still interested in spending time with your friends, but on your own terms.

4. Blame Your Schedule: If you're uncomfortable with being direct, you can use your schedule as an excuse. Saying "I have an early class tomorrow" or "I've got a big project to work on" gives you an easy way out without having to explain yourself too much.

5. Surround Yourself with Like-Minded Friends: One of the best ways to avoid peer pressure is to build a support system of friends who respect your choices. Surround yourself with people who share your values or who, at the very least, won't pressure you to compromise them. Being in an environment that supports your decisions makes it easier to stay true to yourself.

6. Practice Saying No: It can be helpful to rehearse how you'll respond in situations where you feel pressured. Practicing with a friend or in front of a mirror can build your confidence. That way, when the moment comes, you'll know exactly what to say and how to say it.

College is a time of growth and exploration, but it's also important to stay grounded and make decisions that reflect who you truly are. Learning how to handle peer pressure with confidence and grace will empower you to make choices that are best for your health, happiness, and future. Remember, true friends will respect your boundaries, and staying true to yourself is always the best choice.

EXAMPLE SCENARIOS FOR TEENAGERS

- **Pressure to Skip Studying for a Social Event:** Let's say your friends invite you to a party the night before a big exam but you know you need to study; it can be tough to say no. Try explaining your reasons honestly "I really need to focus on my exam tomorrow, but I'd love to hang out another time." True friends will respect your decision, and you'll feel good knowing you prioritized your responsibilities.
- **Pressure to Try Smoking:** If a group of friends offers you a cigarette and you're not comfortable with it, it's important to stick to your values. You can say "No thanks, I'm good," or "Not my thing." Having a simple response ready makes it easier to stay firm, and over time, people will respect your boundaries.

3. Navigating Parties and Social Events Safely

Parties and social events are a common part of college life, offering opportunities to make new friends, unwind, and have fun. However, it's important to approach these events with a mindset of safety and awareness. College parties can sometimes involve risky behaviors like excessive drinking, drug use, or peer pressure, so knowing how to navigate them safely is key to having a good time while protecting your well-being.

Whether it's your first college party or just a casual get-together, being prepared can help you feel more confident in making smart choices. Here are some strategies to ensure you enjoy social events responsibly and stay safe.

Strategies for Navigating Parties Safely

1. Go with Friends You Trust: Arriving at a party with people you trust creates a sense of security. Make a plan to stick together and look out for each other. If someone starts to feel uncomfortable or needs to leave, having a friend nearby makes it easier to exit the situation safely.

2. Set Personal Limits: If you choose to drink, set your own limits before you go. Know how much you're comfortable drinking, and stick to it. You don't have to drink to fit in, and it's okay to say no. If you're not drinking, be confident in your choice – there are many others who will respect that decision.

3. Keep an Eye on Your Drink: Always watch your drink and never leave it unattended. It's a simple way to protect yourself from unwanted substances being added to your drink. If you need to step away, take your drink with you or get a new one when you return.

4. Pace Yourself: If you're drinking, take your time. Sipping your drink slowly helps you stay in control and aware of how much alcohol you're consuming. Remember that the effects of alcohol take time to set in, so give yourself a moment to see how you're feeling before having another.

5. Know When to Leave: Trust your instincts. If the vibe at the party shifts or you feel uncomfortable, it's okay to leave early. You don't have to stay at a party if it doesn't feel right. Having a plan for transportation – whether it's a rideshare app or a designated driver – ensures you can leave safely whenever you're ready.

6. Have a Backup Plan: It's always smart to have a backup plan, like a trusted friend you can call if you need help or an emergency contact who knows where you are. Having a safety net makes navigating social situations feel less daunting.

College parties can be a great way to socialize, but it's essential to prioritize your safety. By setting boundaries, staying with trusted friends, and following your instincts, you can enjoy social events while protecting your well-being. Always remember: it's okay to leave, say no, or skip a party altogether if it doesn't align with your comfort or safety.

EXAMPLE SCENARIOS FOR TEENAGERS

- **Going to a Party with Friends:** When attending a party, make sure you go with friends you trust and plan to stick together. It's easy to get separated in a crowded space, so agree on a meeting point in case anyone gets lost and make sure your phone is charged.
- **Dealing with Uncomfortable Situations:** If someone at a party is making you uncomfortable or pressuring you to do something you're not okay with, trust your instincts. Excuse yourself and find your friends or leave the situation. Having a friend check-in system or code word can help you communicate quickly if you need support.

9. Sexual Health and Healthy Relationships

Navigating relationships and understanding sexual health are important aspects of your college experience. This chapter focuses on building healthy, respectful relationships through open communication and clear boundaries. I'll explore the critical topics of consent, how to communicate effectively with partners, and the importance of maintaining boundaries in romantic relationships. You'll also learn about sexually transmitted diseases (STDs) and safe practices to protect your health. By gaining knowledge and fostering healthy relationships, you can make informed decisions that prioritize your well-being. Let's dive into these essential topics to help you navigate this important part of life with confidence and respect.

1. Consent and Communication

Navigating relationships in college is an important part of growing up, and understanding consent and communication is essential to building healthy, respectful connections. Whether you're in a casual or serious relationship, knowing how to express your boundaries and listen to others' boundaries is key to creating mutual trust, respect, and understanding. Consent is not just about saying "yes" or "no" to sexual activity – it's about open, ongoing communication in all aspects of relationships.

Consent is an agreement between people, made freely and clearly, where both parties understand and respect each other's boundaries. It must be enthusiastic, mutual, and continuous – meaning it can be revoked at any time. Consent is also specific, so agreeing to one activity doesn't mean agreeing to everything.

BUILDING CONSENT AND COMMUNICATION SKILLS

1. Ask for Consent Clearly: Consent is more than just asking "Is this okay?" It's about having open and honest conversations about what each person feels comfortable with. Ask clearly and listen to the answer. If the answer isn't enthusiastic, it's important to stop and check in. A non-verbal cue, such as pulling away, also signals discomfort and should be respected.

2. Communicate Openly and Respectfully: Good communication is at the heart of any healthy relationship. Being able to talk about boundaries, desires, and expectations openly ensures that both people feel heard and respected. Whether discussing feelings, setting boundaries, or resolving a conflict, always approach the conversation with kindness and empathy.

3. Respect Personal Boundaries: Everyone has different comfort levels, and respecting those boundaries is crucial. If someone says "no" or seems unsure, it's essential to respect their decision without pressure or judgment. Consent should never be assumed; it should always be clearly expressed and freely given.

4. Understand That Consent Can Be Withdrawn: Consent is ongoing, which means someone can change their mind at any time. If your partner withdraws consent, respect their decision immediately, and don't try to change their mind. The most important thing is creating a safe and respectful environment where both parties feel comfortable.

5. Be Honest About Your Feelings: If something makes you uncomfortable, speak up. Being honest about your feelings, both positive and negative, allows for deeper understanding in relationships. Your partner should also feel comfortable doing the same.

In college, as you explore relationships and personal connections, understanding consent and maintaining open communication are crucial for fostering healthy, respectful relationships. By prioritizing mutual understanding and respect, you can ensure that all your interactions are grounded in trust and care.

EXAMPLE SCENARIOS FOR TEENAGERS

- **Respecting Boundaries in Relationships:** Let's say you're at a party, and someone you're talking to leans in for a kiss. Before moving forward, ask "Is this okay with you?" Checking in ensures that both of you feel comfortable and respected, emphasizing the importance of clear consent in any romantic or physical interaction.
- **Communicating Comfort Zones:** You're in a new relationship, and your partner suggests spending the night together. You feel unsure and decide to express your feelings by saying "I'm not ready for that yet." Open, honest communication helps build trust and ensures that both partners feel safe and understood.

2. Understanding STDs and Safe Practices

As you begin to navigate relationships in college, understanding sexually transmitted diseases (STDs) and how to practice safe sex is crucial for protecting your health and the health of your partners. STDs, also called sexually transmitted infections (STIs), are infections passed from one person to another through sexual contact. Many STDs can be treated with medication, but some can cause long-term health issues if left untreated. Learning about safe practices can help prevent these infections and empower you to make informed choices about your sexual health.

What are STDs?

STDs can be caused by bacteria, viruses, or parasites. Some of the most common include chlamydia, gonorrhea, herpes, human papillomavirus (HPV), and HIV (human immunodeficiency virus). Many STDs don't always show symptoms, making it possible to have and spread an infection without knowing it. That's why regular testing and practicing safe sex are so important.

Tips for Practicing Safe Sex

1. Use Condoms Consistently: Condoms are one of the most effective ways to prevent the spread of STDs. Whether you're using external (male) condoms or internal (female) condoms, they act as a barrier to reduce the risk of transmission during vaginal, anal, or oral sex. Make sure to use a new condom every time and follow the instructions for proper use.

2. Get Tested Regularly: Since STDs can be asymptomatic, regular testing is essential, especially if you're sexually active with multiple partners or in a new relationship. Most college health centers offer free or low-cost testing, and it's a good idea to discuss testing with your partner(s) before becoming sexually active.

3. Communicate Openly with Your Partner: Talking about sexual health with your partner can feel uncomfortable, but open communication is key to protecting both of you. Discuss past sexual history, STD testing, and safe sex practices before engaging in sexual activity.

4. Limit the Number of Sexual Partners: Reducing the number of sexual partners can lower your risk of being exposed to an STD. If you're in a relationship, consider discussing whether both partners will be exclusive and make sure both of you are regularly tested.

5. Get Vaccinated: Some STDs, like HPV, can be prevented with vaccines. It's a good idea to check with your healthcare provider about vaccines that can protect you from certain infections.

Understanding STDs and practicing safe sex is a vital part of managing your sexual health in college. By taking proactive steps like using condoms, getting tested, and communicating with your partner, you can protect yourself and your relationships, ensuring that your sexual experiences are enjoyable, healthy, and safe.

EXAMPLE SCENARIOS FOR TEENAGERS

- **Discussing Safe Practices with a Partner:** You're in a relationship and decide to become sexually active. Before moving forward, you and your partner talk about using condoms to protect against STDs. Even if it's awkward, having this conversation ensures you're both being responsible and prioritizing each other's health.
- **Getting Tested Together:** You and your partner want to make sure you're both healthy, so you decide to visit a clinic for STD testing together. Regular testing is an important step in staying informed and preventing the spread of infections, even if neither of you has symptoms. It's a way to show mutual responsibility and commitment to safety.

3. Maintaining Boundaries in Romantic Relationships

Maintaining healthy boundaries in romantic relationships is essential for your emotional well-being and for building respectful, lasting connections. College is a time when many people explore new relationships, but it's also a time to develop the skills to maintain those relationships in a way that honors your needs and values. Clear, respectful boundaries help ensure that both partners feel safe, heard, and respected, while also preventing misunderstandings and emotional strain.

Why Boundaries Matter

Boundaries define what is acceptable in a relationship, from physical and emotional space to personal values and needs. Setting boundaries allows you to communicate what you're comfortable with and ensures that both you and your partner are on the same page. This creates a foundation of trust, respect, and mutual understanding, which are all critical components of a healthy relationship.

Tips for Maintaining Boundaries in College Relationships

1. Know What You Want and Need: Before you can set boundaries, it's important to understand your own needs, both emotionally and physically. Reflect on what makes you feel safe, respected, and comfortable. This could involve your preferences for time spent together, physical affection, or how you handle disagreements.

2. Communicate Clearly and Early: Open communication is key to maintaining boundaries. Be clear and direct about your needs and expectations early in the relationship. Whether it's about how much time you want to spend together or what you're comfortable with physically, sharing your feelings honestly can prevent confusion later on.

3. Respect Your Partner's Boundaries: Boundaries are a two-way street. Just as you expect your partner to respect your limits, it's equally important to honor theirs. Listen carefully when your partner expresses their needs, and be mindful of their comfort zones.

4. Check In Regularly: Relationships are dynamic, and boundaries can change over time. It's helpful to have regular check-ins with your partner to ensure that both of you are still comfortable with the boundaries in place. These discussions can deepen your connection and ensure that your relationship remains healthy and respectful.

5. Say No When Needed: It's okay to say no in a relationship. Whether it's turning down an activity you're not comfortable with or needing space for yourself, your partner should respect your right to decline without pressure or guilt.

Maintaining boundaries in a romantic relationship is about protecting your well-being and fostering mutual respect. By knowing your needs, communicating openly, and checking in regularly, you can build a relationship that supports your personal growth and emotional health while ensuring that both you and your partner feel valued and respected.

EXAMPLE SCENARIOS FOR TEENAGERS

- **Setting Boundaries Early:** You've started dating someone new and feel the relationship is progressing fast. Have a conversation about what you're comfortable with, making it clear that you need time before taking any big steps. Open communication helps maintain respect and trust in the relationship.
- **Respecting Each Other's Space:** Between classes, clubs, and friends, you and your partner are busy. Together, agree to set aside time for each other while also making sure to keep space for personal activities. Balancing time together and apart strengthens your relationship and shows that you respect each other's needs.

10. Preparing for Post-College Life

As college comes to a close, the transition into post-college life brings new challenges and opportunities. This chapter is designed to help you prepare for life beyond graduation by focusing on long-term health and well-being. I'll discuss the importance of creating sustainable health habits, managing the stress that comes with newfound independence, and planning for the future with tools like health insurance and wellness apps. By developing these skills now, you'll be better equipped to navigate the demands of adult life while prioritizing your physical and mental health. Let's explore how to set yourself up for a healthy and successful future.

1. Creating Long-term Health Habits

Creating long-term health habits in college is one of the best investments you can make for your future. As you navigate the challenges and opportunities of college life, the habits you develop now will not only support your physical and mental well-being but will also set the foundation for a healthy lifestyle beyond graduation. Building these habits might seem daunting with a busy schedule, but small, consistent changes can lead to lasting benefits.

Why Building Health Habits Now Matters

College is a time of significant transition, and it's easy to prioritize academics, social activities, and other responsibilities over self-care. However, forming healthy habits early on can prevent burnout, reduce stress, and improve your overall quality of life. Whether it's staying active, eating well, or managing stress, the key is to start small and stay consistent.

Strategies for Building Long-Term Health Habits

1. Prioritize Sleep: College students often sacrifice sleep to meet academic or social demands, but quality rest is crucial for maintaining physical and mental health. Aim for seven to nine hours of sleep each night. Establish a bedtime routine that helps you wind down, like limiting screen time before bed or practicing relaxation techniques. Consistent, restful sleep will help you stay focused and energized throughout the day.

2. Stay Physically Active: Incorporating regular physical activity into your routine can boost your mood, increase energy, and improve overall health. Even with a tight schedule, find ways to move your body, whether it's through a morning walk, joining a campus fitness class, or taking the stairs instead of the elevator. Small, frequent bursts of movement can be just as beneficial as longer workouts.

3. Develop Mindful Eating Habits: Eating healthy in college doesn't have to be complicated. Focus on balancing your meals with a variety of foods, including fruits, vegetables, proteins, and whole grains. Listen to your body's hunger and fullness cues and aim to avoid emotional eating. Making thoughtful choices around food will help you feel better in both the short and long term.

4. Manage Stress Effectively: Stress is a common part of college life, but learning how to manage it is key to preventing burnout. Practice mindfulness, meditation, or yoga to stay grounded during stressful times. Regular breaks, journaling, and spending time with friends can also help reduce stress levels.

5. Make Health a Lifelong Commitment: The habits you form in college will continue to influence your health after graduation. Stay consistent with your sleep, exercise, and nutrition routines even as your life changes. Remember that health is a long-term investment – what you do now impacts your well-being years from now.

By focusing on these small, manageable habits, you'll not only thrive during college but also set yourself up for a healthy, balanced life after graduation.

Example Scenarios

- **Establishing a Consistent Workout Routine:** As you transition from college to post-college life, maintaining regular physical activity can be challenging. Start by scheduling a simple workout routine that fits your lifestyle, like a twenty-minute walk after work or a weekly fitness class. Making exercise a regular part of your schedule will help you stay active and energized in your new routine.
- **Building Healthy Eating Habits:** When you start living on your own, it's easy to rely on convenience foods. However, making a habit of preparing simple, balanced meals can greatly impact your health in the long run. Plan your meals

ahead of time, focusing on fruits, vegetables, and whole grains, to create sustainable, healthy eating habits that you can maintain for years to come.

2. Transitioning to Independence: Managing Stress

Transitioning to independence, whether during college or after graduation, is an exciting yet challenging time. As you take on more responsibilities and learn to navigate life on your own, it's common to experience stress. Managing stress effectively during this transition is essential for your overall well-being and success. With the right tools and mindset, you can handle the pressures of independence while maintaining a sense of balance and calm.

Understanding the Causes of Stress

As you become more independent, stress can come from various sources: academic pressures, financial responsibilities, balancing social life with personal commitments, and adjusting to living away from home. It's important to recognize that stress is a normal part of this process. However, when it becomes overwhelming, it can affect your mental and physical health, making it harder to stay focused and enjoy your college or post-college experience.

Strategies for Managing Stress During the Transition

1. Create a Routine: A daily routine can provide structure and reduce the uncertainty that often causes stress. Schedule time for studying, work, socializing, and self-care activities like exercise or relaxation. Having a plan helps you stay organized and ensures that you make time for things that reduce stress.

2. Set Realistic Goals: One of the main sources of stress is setting expectations that are too high. Break large tasks into smaller, manageable steps, and focus on achieving them one at a time. Celebrate your accomplishments along the way, no matter how small they may seem. Setting realistic, achievable goals can reduce anxiety and help you stay motivated.

3. Learn to Say No: As you take on new responsibilities, it's important to understand your limits. Saying yes to every opportunity can lead to burnout. Prioritize your well-being by saying no to activities or commitments that might overextend your energy and time. Recognize that it's okay to focus on what matters most to you.

4. Develop Coping Mechanisms: Find healthy ways to cope with stress, such as practicing mindfulness, deep breathing exercises, or journaling. Engaging in hobbies you enjoy, spending time with supportive friends, and staying active can also help you relieve tension and refocus.

5. Ask for Help When Needed: Transitioning to independence doesn't mean you have to go it alone. Reach out to family, friends, mentors, or campus counselors when you're feeling overwhelmed. Talking about your feelings and challenges can help you gain perspective and find solutions.

Managing stress during this time of change is essential for building resilience and confidence as you transition into adulthood. With a few simple strategies, you can maintain balance, embrace new responsibilities, and enjoy the process of becoming independent.

Example Scenarios

- **Balancing Work and Life:** After landing your first job post-college, you feel overwhelmed with the new responsibilities. To manage your stress, set boundaries by turning off work notifications after hours and dedicating weekends to relaxing activities, like hiking or reading. This will help you recharge and maintain a healthier work-life balance.
- **Managing Financial Stress:** Now that you've graduated from college, you're responsible for rent, bills, and student loan payments. To reduce stress, create a budget that includes

essentials, savings, and fun money. Tracking your spending will keep you in control of your finances and help you avoid the anxiety of unexpected expenses.

3. Planning for the Future: Health Insurance and Wellness Apps

As you prepare to transition from college into the next phase of your life, planning for your future health and well-being becomes increasingly important. After graduation, one of the key areas to focus on is managing your health responsibly, and this includes securing health insurance and utilizing wellness apps to support your physical and mental well-being.

HEALTH INSURANCE: A VITAL INVESTMENT

Once you're no longer covered by your parents' insurance plan or a college health plan, finding the right health insurance is essential. While it might seem complicated, understanding your options can save you from unexpected medical costs and ensure you receive the necessary care.

1. Explore Coverage Options: If you land a full-time job, check to see if your employer offers health insurance as part of your benefits package. Employer-sponsored insurance often comes with lower premiums and comprehensive coverage. If you're freelancing or in between jobs, look into purchasing your own health insurance through government marketplaces or private providers. Don't forget to consider Medicaid (a government program that provides free or low-cost health insurance to people with low income) if your income qualifies you for it.

2. Compare Plans: When choosing a plan, compare the coverage options carefully. Focus on what's important for your situation – whether it's prescription coverage, specialist visits, or mental health services. Make sure you understand the plan's premiums, deductibles, and copays to ensure it fits your budget.

3. Don't Delay: It's easy to put off health insurance if you're healthy, but accidents and illnesses can happen unexpectedly. Having insurance can prevent costly medical bills and give you peace of mind that you're protected when you need it most.

Wellness Apps: Tools for Maintaining Health

In today's digital world, wellness apps can be valuable tools for maintaining both your physical and mental health. Many are free or inexpensive and can help you build and sustain healthy habits, even after college.

1. Fitness and Nutrition Apps: Apps like MyFitnessPal, Nike Training Club, or Fitbit can help you track your fitness goals, monitor your nutrition, and encourage regular exercise. These apps provide structure, track progress, and keep you motivated.

2. Mental Health Apps: For managing stress, anxiety, or even tracking your mood, apps like Headspace or Calm offer meditation guides, breathing exercises, and sleep support. They can be a great way to manage mental health in your daily life.

3. Health Management Apps: Apps like Zocdoc or GoodRx can help you find doctors, manage appointments, and locate affordable prescriptions. Having these tools handy ensures you stay on top of your health care.

Planning for your future health through insurance and wellness apps ensures that you're taking proactive steps to maintain your well-being in the years ahead. These resources make it easier to manage your health independently, so you can focus on living well after college.

Example Scenarios

- **Exploring Health Insurance Options:** After graduating, you'll lose access to student health services. If you're starting a job, check whether your employer offers health insurance and what the plan covers. If not, look into affordable options like staying on your parents' plan until you turn twenty-six or using

a marketplace like Healthcare.gov. Don't wait until you need medical care to figure out coverage – it's better to plan ahead!
- **Using Wellness Apps:** You just graduated and are adjusting to post-college life. To keep up with your health, download a wellness app to track your daily exercise, sleep, and stress levels. The app's reminders will help you stay consistent with self-care, making it easier to maintain healthy habits as you plan for the future.

Conclusion: Staying Healthy for the Long Run

As you reach the end of this guide, it's important to pause and reflect on your wellness journey. College is a time of tremendous growth, both academically and personally, and managing your health throughout this period is a crucial part of that experience. From your first steps as a freshman to your final year, each stage presents its own challenges and opportunities for learning. The habits and knowledge you've gained along the way will serve as a foundation for a lifetime of well-being. This is your moment to take stock of what you've learned, how far you've come, and how you can continue to prioritize your health in the years ahead.

Reflecting on Your Wellness Journey

When you think back on your time in college, you'll realize that staying healthy isn't just about physical fitness or eating right. It's about a holistic approach that includes mental, emotional, and relational well-being. You've navigated countless new experiences, learned to balance academic pressures, managed relationships, and maybe even faced setbacks along the way. Each of these moments contributes to your overall health journey.

By building a hygiene routine, you've set the foundation for self-care that will carry you through the rigors of daily life. Learning to eat for energy and wellness has shown you how food can be a powerful tool for both your body and mind. Understanding basic medical knowledge has empowered you to take charge of your health, while emotional management and mental health strategies have given you the tools to handle stress, anxiety, and the pressures that come with being a student.

Your relationships, both romantic and platonic, have played a critical role in shaping your college experience. Whether it's managing friendships or navigating romantic boundaries, these relationships have taught you the importance of clear communication, empathy, and respect. Additionally, learning to balance digital health with real-world interactions has helped you create healthier habits around technology, which is essential in today's fast-paced, screen-driven world.

Perhaps most importantly, you've developed strategies for balancing academics and wellness – an ongoing challenge for many students. Understanding that your mental and physical health are just as important as your GPA is a vital lesson that will continue to serve you well. And, as you prepare to transition into post-college life, you now have the tools to make informed decisions about alcohol, drugs, and sexual health, among others, ensuring you stay safe and make choices that align with your values.

Continuing Healthy Habits Beyond College

While college may be a unique time in your life, the habits you've formed don't end at graduation. In fact, the wellness practices you've cultivated will become even more crucial as you enter the next phase of your life, whether you're starting a job, continuing your education, or embarking on a new adventure. Transitioning into the "real world" brings a new set of challenges, but the self-awareness and knowledge you've gained will help you navigate them.

One of the most important things you can do moving forward is to continue the healthy habits you've developed in college. This means sticking to a regular hygiene routine, maintaining a balanced diet, and finding ways to incorporate physical activity into your daily life, even when your schedule gets busy. It's easy to let these habits slide when faced with the demands of work or adult responsibilities, but consistency is key to long-term health.

Your mental and emotional health are just as important after college as they were during it. Life's pressures don't disappear when you graduate; they simply evolve. Continue practicing the emotional management techniques you've learned, such as mindfulness, journaling, or seeking support when needed. Keep nurturing the relationships that matter to you, and don't hesitate to seek professional help if you find yourself struggling with your mental health. Being proactive about your well-being is a sign of strength, not weakness.

As you move into the next chapter of your life, remember that health is a lifelong journey. It's not about perfection – it's about making choices that support your overall well-being, one day at a time. You may face new obstacles, but the resilience and self-care habits you've built during your college years will help you handle whatever comes your way.

A Final Thought

Your college experience has been about more than just earning a degree – it's been a time of self-discovery, growth, and learning how to take care of yourself in a holistic way. The strategies you've gained in building a hygiene routine, eating for health and energy, managing relationships, and balancing academics and wellness are not just for your college years – they are tools that will help you thrive for the rest of your life.

As you step into the world beyond college, know that your health and wellness are ongoing priorities. Continue to reflect on your journey, stay committed to your well-being, and take pride in the fact that you've equipped yourself with the knowledge and habits necessary for a healthy, fulfilling life. This guide may be ending, but your wellness journey is just beginning. Stay curious, stay compassionate with yourself, and always remember: your health is your most valuable asset.

Thanks for Reading!

I hope you found *College Student Health Guide - Managing Wellness from Freshman Year to Graduation* helpful as you prepare for this exciting new chapter. Supporting you in maintaining both physical and mental well-being is my goal, and I'm so glad I could be a part of your journey.

As someone who has seen firsthand the challenges that come with transitioning to college life, I wanted to create a resource that parents can trust and students can rely on. This guide was written with care and thoughtfulness, keeping in mind all the stresses and joys of this important time in life.

Your feedback is incredibly important to me and to future readers. By leaving a review, you're not only helping me improve, but also assisting other students and families in choosing a guide that meets their needs. Simply scan the QR code below to share your thoughts on Amazon. Your honest review would mean so much!

Thank you for trusting this book as part of your college journey. Wishing you all the best in health, growth, and success!

— Jules Carson